THEY
NEVER KNEW

THEY
NEVER KNEW

THE
VICTIMS
OF
NUCLEAR
TESTING

BY GLENN CHENEY

AN IMPACT BOOK
FRANKLIN WATTS
A DIVISION OF GROLIER PUBLISHING
NEW YORK   LONDON   HONG KONG   SYDNEY
DANBURY, CONNECTICUT

Library of Congress Cataloging–in–Publication Data

Cheney, Glenn Alan.
    They never knew : the victims of nuclear testing / by Glenn
Cheney.
        p. cm.
    Includes bibliographical references and index.
    Summary: Examines the American government's role in develop-
ing nuclear weapons and conducting atomic testing, focusing on the
effects of radiation on humans and the victims' attempts to sue the
government for compensation.
    ISBN 0-531-11273-X
    1. Nuclear warfare—Health aspects. 2. Nuclear weapons—
Testing—Health aspects. [Nuclear warfare—Health aspects. 2.
Nuclear weapons—Testing—Health aspects. 3. Radiation victims.]
I. Title.
RA648.3C475   1996
363.17'992'0973—dc20   96-14262 CIP AC

CONTENTS

INTRODUCTION
7

ONE
THE BOMB AND THE EFFECTS
OF RADIATION
12

TWO
THE BOMB AND THE COLD WAR,
1945–1950
22

THREE
TESTING IN NEVADA
35

FOUR
ATOMIC TESTING AND THE
PEOPLE NEARBY
51

FIVE
THE MYSTERY OF THE SHEEP
62

SIX
THE DISASTROUS EFFECTS ON HEALTH
71

SEVEN
THE PEOPLE VS. THE AEC IN COURT
88

EIGHT
TREATIES TOWARD A TEST BAN
105

GLOSSARY   110
SUGGESTED READING   114
SOURCE NOTES   116
INDEX   125

INTRODUCTION

One hundred and forty-nine atomic bombs have exploded over America.[1] No one knows how many people these bombs have killed. The initial heat and shock of the explosions probably killed no one. Open-air atomic explosions, however, have more—lasting and—distant effects. They create and release tremendous amounts of highly dangerous radioactive materials. Radiation causes leukemia and other forms of cancer, cardiovascular problems, cataracts, immunological weaknesses, genetic defects, prenatal problems, mental retardation, and many other health problems. Such problems, however, occur only years or decades after the explosions. All doctors and scientists can do is estimate the number of the problems and the number of probable deaths. Estimates of deaths worldwide from American, Soviet, British, French, and Chinese atmospheric nuclear tests range from something near zero to several million.[2]

In the name of democracy and self-defense, the United States tested bomb after bomb at a test site in Nevada. Each shot sent tons of radioactive particles boiling into the sky and drifting across the United States. Uranium, plutonium, cesium, strontium, iodine, and other radioactive forms of elements gradually came to earth as fallout. A lot of the fallout settled in Nevada and Utah, killing cattle and sickening residents. It caused burns on ranchers' skin, leukemia in children, cancer in adults, and deformities in the unborn. It contaminated milk in North Dakota.[3] It ruined photographic film in New York. It settled into the soil of every state except Alaska and Hawaii.[4]

Another sixty-six test bombs—many of them far more powerful than those in Nevada, were detonated over the Marshall Islands, a U.S. Trusteeship territory in the South Pacific. An estimated 5,000 local people had to abandon their homes and live for four decades on distant islands. Some 42,000 U.S. military personnel trying to clean up the atomic mess worked under conditions so radioactive that they would be illegal in any American industry today.[5]

In all, almost half a million Americans have had an atomic bomb, or several, explode near enough to do them harm. How many have these bombs killed? After years of lies and denial, the United States government reluctantly admitted to a toll of perhaps a dozen civilians. Although thousands of American citizens have sued the government, claiming damages that range from illness to death, few have received compensation. These lawsuits have been generally unsuccessful because among other reasons, it is difficult—perhaps impossible—to establish a definite link between illnesses like cancer and explosions that happened hundreds of miles away and ten or twenty or forty years in the past.

Scientists, among them several Nobel laureates, have warned that the radiation from atomic bomb tests may eventually cause as many as 10 million deaths worldwide. Other scientists claim the fallout was so dispersed and diluted by air and water that it could not be harmful.

The U.S. Congress investigated the claims. It found negligence in the testing program and horrifying consequences. U.S. courts, however, have very rarely awarded compensation to those who claim to have been injured by radiation from the tests.

Among the victims are an unknown number of the 250,000 military personnel who witnessed atomic explosions or their aftermath during training for nuclear warfare. Used as human guinea pigs, they were ordered into positions as close as 1.2 miles (1.9 km) from atomic explosions so that the military would learn the effects of radiation on their physical and mental health. Some were used as human robots to gather information near ground zero or in radioactive clouds. Some soldiers were protected by nothing more than a trench dug 6 feet (1.8 m) deep and perhaps sunglasses or a cotton face mask. All this while scientists and officers hid in specially protected bomb shelters many miles away.

Bombs were not the only source of exposure to radiation. A government research program had hospital patients injected with plutonium, one of the deadliest substances in the world.[6] Some 16,000 people were subjected to experiments involving radiation, many of them unaware of the nature of the experiment or the real degree of danger.

No one will ever know the whole truth. Information was hidden by the Atomic Energy Commission (AEC) and other government agencies. Much of the available information has been distorted by hysteria, rumor, and wild fears.

The tests may have been dangerous, but they took place during dangerous times. A war in Korea was in the process of killing tens of thousands of U.S. troops. The Soviet Union, an avowed enemy of the United States, was developing a nuclear arsenal that very quickly became powerful enough to destroy every city in North America. In the infancy and adolescence of nuclear science, bombs, designs, fuels, and triggers had to be tested. If the United States had let the Soviet Union get ahead in the design or production of atomic weapons, the weakness of the U.S. arsenal might very well have tempted the Soviets to launch a nuclear war. Atomic testing, therefore, in one place or another, was necessary to maintain a balance of power. Ironically, American bombs were exploded only in American territory, and, if we include the people of the Marshall Islands, the only people killed were Americans. It was almost as if the U.S. had unleashed a nuclear war on itself.

Twenty years after the tests stopped, Americans started asking questions. Did the program have to be carried out in such secrecy? Did the AEC have to deny the dangers of fallout? Could it not have announced upcoming tests? Could it not have warned the public about approaching clouds of radiation and the link between radiation and cancer?

The important issue here is not the tests themselves as much as the behavior of the U.S. government. It is now generally acknowledged that government agents and agencies denied the known danger of radiation, lied to the public about the safety of the tests, perjured themselves in court, withheld information that would have indicated guilt, falsified records that indicated problems, and discouraged research that might have revealed the danger of testing.[7]

Though the lesson has been learned about the dangers of exploding nuclear weapons in earth's atmosphere, more must be known about the effects of radiation, not just from bombs but from nuclear power, nuclear waste, nuclear medicine, and equipment that uses nuclear materials. At the same time, questions remain. How well does the government regulate its own activities and judge its own negligence? Also, what are the long-term repercussions of working with new technologies? In short, we need to learn how to live in the nuclear age. A look at the past, therefore, may offer a glimpse of our future.

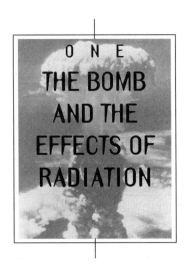

O N E

THE BOMB AND THE EFFECTS OF RADIATION

The core of a fission bomb, which is commonly referred to as an atomic bomb (or A-bomb), is a few kilos of nuclear fuel, either uranium or plutonium. The bomb that destroyed Hiroshima had about 12 kilotons of plutonium fuel. Today, 3 kilotons would be enough for a small bomb, and a high-tech device could detonate as little as 1 kiloton to produce the explosive power of 1,000 tons of TNT.[1]

To explode, the fuel must begin a chain reaction within itself. In a fission bomb, that chain reaction is caused by a radioactive atom splitting apart. When it splits, neutrons shoot out to split more atoms. Those atoms in turn release more neutrons. The chain reaction, known as fission, expands extremely rapidly, with each split atom releasing a tremendous amount of energy, which is an atomic explosion.

The chain reaction begins when the fuel reaches critical mass, that is, a given amount of fuel that is compressed to a certain density. For an atomic explosion to occur, the fuel must be compressed very quickly. If it doesn't occur quickly enough, the chain reaction causes a small explosion that simply throws the fuel apart, relieving it from critical mass. Once the fuel is separated, the chain reaction stops. Such a small, subnuclear explosion, however, is dangerous because it throws the radioactive fuel into the air.

To serve as the core of a bomb, the fuel is formed into a sphere and is surrounded by a normal chemical explosive. An electrical charge distributed to various points of that explosive shell detonates all of the chemical explosive at precisely the same moment. The chemical explosion forces the nuclear fuel inward, achieving critical mass and, if everything has been designed and built just right, an atomic explosion.

A fusion bomb, or hydrogen bomb (or H-bomb), is a little more complicated. While the fission process is a process of splitting up atoms, the fusion process is the combining of hydrogen atoms to form helium atoms. A lot of energy is needed to force that combination. The combination, however, releases even more energy. Only a fission explosion is powerful enough to start a fusion reaction.

Hydrogen bombs, then, are, in part, fission bombs. A chemical explosion compresses atomic fuel enough to touch off a fission explosion. This in turn infuses enough energy into the core of the hydrogen bomb to cause it to go into fusion, releasing an enormous explosion.

The efficiency and yield of atomic weapons depend on many factors. The triggering device that detonates the chemical explosion determines how much of the core is compressed to critical mass before the explosion throws it apart. The chemical explosive itself needs to be tested for efficiency. The nuclear fuel, too, needs to be tested. If the bomb is tested in the atmosphere, that is, above ground, the test includes an observation of the radioactive cloud. Detonation at different altitudes creates different amounts of radioactive material. Weather determines the shape and altitude of the explosion, where the radioactive cloud drifts, and the pattern of its radioactive fallout.

When atoms are split by the fission process, they form new atoms, some of which are radioactive. Scientists study fallout to learn about what happened in the atomic explosion. By analyzing the isotopes (*see* "The Nature of Radiation," below) scattered across the ground or water surface and through the air, they can determine how much of the fuel actually exploded. Typically it is only 2 to 3 percent. The rest gets thrown into the air.

The power of the atomic explosion, also referred to as its yield, is measured in kilotons (kt) or megatons (mt). A *kiloton* is the explosive equivalent of 1,000 tons of TNT. A *megaton* equals 1,000,000 tons of TNT. The bomb at Hiroshima had a yield of about 13 kilotons. The Nagasaki bomb yielded 23 kilotons. In 1961, the Soviet Union tested a hydrogen bomb that yielded over 50 megatons, sending up a cloud so vast and radioactive that Americans were warned not to eat fresh food for a few days. Scientists have theorized that there is no limit to the potential yield of a hydrogen bomb.

THE NATURE OF RADIATION

Radiation occurs when certain atoms lose or gain protons to form different atoms. In the process, subatomic particles and electromagnetic waves shoot out from the atom's nucleus. Those emissions are radiation.

A given element always has a certain number of protons, but the number of neutrons can vary. Each variation in number of neutrons is called an *isotope* of that element. Two common isotopes of uranium are uranium-235 and uranium-238. (The number is the isotope's mass number, or its total number of protons and neutrons.) In the case of radioactive elements, some isotopes are more radioactive than others.

Uranium-235 and plutonium-239 are the common fuels for atomic weapons. To be of weapons grade, the uranium or plutonium must be enriched by removing other isotopes and elements until it is about 90 percent pure.

Radiation occurs normally in nature. We are surrounded by what is called background radiation. Eight percent of background radiation showers down on us from outer space, and people who live at higher elevations receive more of this cosmic radiation than people who live at sea level. Decaying radioactive elements deep in the earth send radiation into our basements as radon, which is the source of an average of 55 percent of the radiation around us. Eleven percent of background radiation comes from within our own bodies. About 18 percent of background radiation comes from man-made sources. An average of 15 percent comes from medical applications such as X rays and the like. Less than 0.3 percent comes from fallout. The testing program of the 1950s added the radiation from the atomic reactions to the normal background radiation.[2]

Background radiation is almost certainly responsible for some of the cancers and genetic changes that occur in plants and animals. In fact, it may be responsible for most of the genetic changes that cause evolution. If this is true, then it can be said that life depends on radiation.

Radiation from atomic reactions, be it an explosion or the controlled chain reaction in a nuclear power plant or the gradual decay of nuclear fuel or radioactive elements in medical treatments, is essentially the same as most background radiation. The difference is in intensity. Since radiation was discovered, and especially since it has been created artificially, scientists have been trying to figure out how much radiation is too much.

Radiation comes in four basic forms. *Alpha radiation* occurs when an atom releases an alpha particle, which is composed of two protons and two neutrons, to form a new element. Being relatively large, the alpha particles can be an especially dangerous form of radiation. They lose energy quickly, however, and so they don't travel far and cannot penetrate skin or even a piece of paper. If radioactive particles, or *radionuclides*, releasing alpha radiation manage to enter the human body, however, the alpha particles will inevitably hit tissue and do damage.

Beta radiation is the result of a neutron changing to a proton, or vice versa. This change causes the radioactive atom to change into a different element. During the change, a beta particle is emitted. Beta particles are smaller, lighter, and faster than alpha particles. They can penetrate the skin, but because they go farther through tissue, their effect is less concentrated and thus less dangerous.

Gamma radiation is an electromagnetic wave somewhat like an X ray. It can travel long distances and penetrate not only the human body but even several inches of steel or concrete. Gamma radiation is dangerous because it can affect tissue even if radionuclides are not ingested.

Neutrons are released during fission as heavy radioactive atoms such as uranium and plutonium break into smaller atoms. Like gamma radiation, neutrons travel fast and far with great penetrating power.

Radiation tends to subside as the radioactive atoms break down into nonradioactive elements. A given radioactive atom decays at a random moment, and radiation is released. Where there is a quantity of atoms of a radioactive isotope, the moments occur at a steady average. The rate of decay is measured in terms of its half-life, that is, the time it takes half of the remaining radioactive atoms to decay. The half-life of plutonium-

239 is about 24,000 years, that of uranium-238 about 4 billion years, and that of bismuth-214 under twenty minutes.

Radiation is measured in several ways. Radioactive activity is the number of atoms breaking down per second. One *becquerel* equals one decay per second. The *roentgen* is a unit of radioactive exposure that measures how much radiation is hitting a given spot.

Absorbed dose is an important measurement because it indicates the amount of radiation absorbed by living tissue. The *gray* is the current measurement of absorbed dose. In the past, absorbed dosage was measured by the *rad.* (This book refers to the rad because that was the unit used in the 1950s and is still commonly used outside of scientific circles.) One gray equals 100 rad. Sometimes radiation readings refer to a rad rate, such as "5 rad per hour." One rad tends to equal approximately one roentgen.

Dose equivalent measures the actual effect of radiation on living tissue. Since various forms of radiation have various effects, each form has a quality factor. That factor is multiplied by the gray unit to produce a dose equivalent unit called the *sievert* or, in the past (and in this book), the *rem.* One sievert equals 100 rem.

RADIATION AND HEALTH

Radiation can injure or kill a living cell or influence its reproduction. If cellular damage affects the cell's ability to control its growth, the cell may replicate and spread wildly, a condition known as cancer.

Radiation can also damage a reproductive cell's DNA, changing its genetic code. A fetus with damaged DNA usually dies before birth. If it does survive, the newborn has birth defects that can include serious mental and physical disabilities.

Radiation's effects on health are not as distinct and identifiable as the effects of, say, a bullet or a specific disease. A given dose of radiation will affect different people in different ways. Depending on the level, one person might die of cancer while another person shows no noticeable effects.

At extremely high radiation levels, over 400 rad, the human organism is certainly injured, probably fatally and probably within a matter of days or weeks. The central nervous system is severely damaged, causing nausea, uncontrollable vomiting, disorientation, coma, and eventually death. A high dose damages the gastrointestinal tract, causing hemorrhages, diarrhea, and blood poisoning. Because cells in the intestinal tract may not be able to reproduce, death may occur in a number of weeks. Doses of 50 to 150 rad cause nausea, vomiting, dizziness, and other internal problems, but most of the symptoms tend to clear up in a few weeks. Doses over 100 rad can cause skin burns and loss of hair.

The minimum dose needed to damage the immune system and the DNA of cells seems to depend on the individual who is exposed. Exposure to very low levels—no one is sure how low—can lead to long-term health problems, including cancer, leukemia, cardiovascular illness, and other organic problems. Leukemia tends to develop only after five to seven years. Cancer may not develop for a decade or two.

The effects of radiation are often seen only as statistics. The higher the level of exposure, the greater the number of people affected. Doubling a dose from 100 to 200 rad tends to double (roughly speaking) the number of people affected by the radiation. Scientists have no idea why a certain dose affects some people and not others.

Scientists are also not sure if there is a threshold, a level of exposure below which absolutely no one is affected and which is therefore safe. Research has thus far not led to conclusive results.[3] The question has there-fore generated considerable controversy, with levels considered safe by some scientists being called danger-ous by others.

Some research has indicated that a person's expo-sure to low-dose radiation over a long period of time may be more dangerous than exposure to a sudden burst of radiation that equals the amount accumulated over the long term. Theoretically, the cells killed by the sudden burst are ejected from the body by the immune system, and healthy cells replace them. Lower doses over a longer period, however, will modify the genetic structure of cells without killing them. The cells are then able to reproduce genetic flaws that can go on to cause cancer and other diseases.

Any of the illnesses that can be caused by radiation from atomic explosions can also be caused by other cul-prits. Among the many suspected causes of cancer and birth defects are tobacco smoke, food preservatives, alcohol, electromagnetic waves, chemicals, pesticides, sunlight, radon, inherited genetic tendencies, and dozens of other factors. When a person develops cancer or a baby is born with genetic abnormalities, it is usual-ly impossible to positively identify the cause.[4]

To determine causes of cancer, researchers must look at statistics. For example, they know that nation-wide a certain percentage of people die of leukemia. If the incidence of leukemia is greater than the national average in a neighborhood near a certain factory, it is reasonable to suspect that the cause may be related to emissions from that factory. Surveys of areas near similar factories may confirm or negate the suspicion. Still, the leukemia contracted by some or even all of the people near the factory may have been caused by unknown factors related to the emissions from the factory. It may be impossible to link specific cases or deaths to the fac-tory itself. All scientists can determine is the number of excess cases or excess deaths, that is, the number in excess of the expected average.

These are the kinds of problems encountered in trying to determine who has been killed or injured by atomic testing in Nevada and the South Pacific. The levels of radiation that cause health problems are not known with certainty. Ironically, the two populations most exposed to radiation from these tests were people who did not have other contacts with the common causes of cancer and genetic abnormalities. Both populations are far from industrial pollution. Both had little contact with cigarettes, alcohol, drugs, and caffeine and had lifestyles commonly associated with good health. Rates of cancer and birth defects apparently rose, but the question of whether those higher rates can be linked to radiation has been dealt within legal battles more than by scientific inquiry.

The doses of radiation that nuclear workers and others are allowed to receive have been dropping since the dangers of radiation were discovered. Currently, by the standards of the International Commission on Radiological Protection, nuclear workers may not receive total doses of over 5 rem per year. Other people may not receive over 1 rem. The U.S. Department of Energy has even more restrictive limits for its personnel. Their annual dose may not exceed 0.1 rem.

The debate over the effects of long-term low-dose radiation continues. Research conducted by the U.S. Academy of Science indicates that the level that can cause cancer may be one-fifth to one-seventh of current figures. New statistics and data from Hiroshima and Nagasaki indicate that the harmful effects per dose may be double what was thought. Other studies indicate that the risks may be fifteen times higher than recognized by safety regulations.[5]

How does radiation affect health? The answer determines whether alleged victims of nuclear testing were indeed harmed by their exposure. In some cases, the question is whether the exposure was great enough to cause harm. In others, the question is whether a particular illness can be caused by radiation. In all cases, the question becomes muddled by the influence of politics and economics.

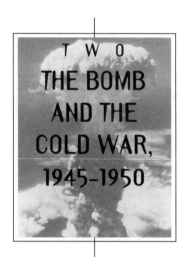

T W O
THE BOMB AND THE COLD WAR, 1945-1950

In the early 1940s, scientists in England and the United States determined that it was theoretically possible to build an atomic bomb. Stronger than their hope of building one was their fear that the German Nazis would do it first. In World War II, German rockets were slamming into London. German submarines were sinking ships off the coast of the United States. German death camps were trying to exterminate every Jew in Europe. The consequences of an atomic weapon in the Nazi arsenal were terrifying beyond the imagination.

Under the administration of President Franklin Roosevelt, the United States began a massive effort to purify uranium and plutonium into nuclear fuel, to design the mechanisms that would make the fuel explode, and to build the bomb and test it. The effort was given a code name, the Manhattan Project, and it was overseen by a secret agency, the Manhattan District, under General Leslie Groves.

By July 1945, just two months after Germany surrendered, an American atomic bomb was ready to test. The possible target, by that time, was the only remaining enemy, Japan.

The bomb had to be tested. No one had ever built or detonated an even remotely similar explosive device. No one knew whether the triggering device would successfully create a critical mass, how big the explosion would be, or what would happen afterward. Some scientists speculated that the chain reaction would go on to split the oxygen and nitrogen atoms of the atmosphere, turning the earth into an intensely bright star that would soon burn itself out.

That first test was code-named Trinity. Manhattan Project scientists and military personnel chose Alamogordo, New Mexico, as the site because of its isolation and dry, predictable weather. They expected radioactive fallout but didn't know how much, how far it would go, or how harmful it would be. Radiation monitors took up positions for miles around the test site, ready to take readings and sound the alarm if their Geiger counters detected too much radiation. There was an evacuation plan, but because of the absolute secrecy, no one in surrounding towns and ranches had been informed of the plan or warned of the test.

The 10-ton plutonium-fuel bomb was hoisted to the top of a 103-foot (31-m) tower. As a cable pulled it upward at about a foot (30 cm) a minute, a pile of mattresses below offered protection if the cable snapped. Scientists retreated to bunkers 10,000 yards (9,140 m) to the north, south, and west to monitor the results of the explosion. The man hooking the electrical detonation wires to the bomb was nervous. A thunderstorm was blowing in, and the day before, distant lightning had tripped the trigger of a similar device.

Although most of the world knew nothing of what was happening at Alamogordo—and would not learn of the existence of the atomic bomb until it was used against Japan—the results of the test were bound to have international repercussions. On the date of the test, July 16, 1945, U.S. president Harry S. Truman was beginning negotiations in Potsdam with Soviet premier Joseph Stalin and British prime minister Winston Churchill to determine whether the Soviet Union would join the war against Japan. Truman needed to know whether he had an atomic trump card up his sleeve.

Manhattan District director General Groves therefore had a serious decision to make. If the thunderstorm collided with the radioactive cloud from the bomb, the rain would bring down the radioactive particles in a relatively small area, contaminating the ground with dangerously high levels of radiation. If the fallout settled over a wider area, the radioactivity would be diluted. It would bring radiation levels barely above the level of normal background radiation.

General Groves, under the pressures of an ongoing war in the Pacific, crucial international negotiations in Europe, fear of sabotage, and the need for absolute secrecy, was inclined to put urgency ahead of safety. As it turned out, the thunderstorm passed, and the bomb was detonated just an hour and a half late, at 5:29:45 A.M. As the explosion shot into the sky with an ungodly roar and a flash of light brighter than the sun, many of the witnesses considered the moment of religious significance. They thought of God, the creation of the universe, the nature of evil, and the future of a world that would never be the same again.

A thousand times hotter than the surface of the sun, the explosion vaporized the steel tower on which it had perched. The fire, smoke, and upswept debris rose 6 miles (almost 10 km) into the sky and drifted northeast at about 10 miles (16 km) per hour. The fallout was heaviest over an area 30 miles (48 km) wide and 100 miles (160 km) long. Radiation levels in the nearest towns were too high for Geiger counters to measure. An undetected piece of the cloud split off and drifted over a ranch, and when fallout settled there, cattle lost hair on their backs and developed blisters in the exposed skin. Their owner said the hair grew back white. Trinity personnel inspected the cattle, bought them for a reasonable price, and took them to the AEC facility at Oak Ridge for observation. No permanent damage or genetic abnormalities developed, or at least none were reported to the public. Descendants of those animals still live at Oak Ridge, an indication that even at that first test, the government was aware of the possibility of radiation causing long-term negative effects on health.

The flash and noise had not gone unnoticed by people within hundreds of miles. To explain it, the Alamogordo army air base issued a news release. It reported a massive explosion of ammunition and fireworks.

The Trinity test set several dangerous precedents for the years of testing that followed. Even after the end of the war, the urgency of international politics often took priority over safety. Shots were detonated despite risky weather conditions, and people within the range of heavy fallout were not notified of upcoming tests or approaching radiative fallout.

The Trinity shot also produced the first probable victim of atomic testing. When General Groves took reporters out to ground zero to show them that there was no danger after the test, he had his driver walk down into the crater. The driver spent half an hour there. Twenty-two years later he died of leukemia. It was later estimated that he had been exposed to over 100 rad, a dangerous dose.

Ten days after the Trinity test, the United States, England, and China demanded Japan's unconditional surrender. On August 6, an atomic bomb was dropped over Hiroshima that detonated in the air, killing, immediately or eventually, somewhere between 100,000 and 180,000 people.[1] (The exact number of eventual deaths directly attributable to the effects of radiation is not known because it is impossible to relate cancer deaths to exposure to carcinogens. See the discussion in Chapter One.) Slow to understand the nature of this new threat, Japan hesitated to surrender. On August 9, another atomic bomb exploded this time over Nagasaki, killing an estimated 70,000. Surrender came two days later. World War II was over, and its survivors stood blinking in the blinding light of the nuclear age.

THE FIRST ATOMIC VETERANS—HIROSHIMA AND NAGASAKI

A few days after the explosion, the first Americans to arrive in Hiroshima were prisoners of war from a nearby prison camp, brought in to help clean up debris. They, of course, had no idea what had caused such dreadful devastation and assumed that the outlines of human forms on streets and sidewalks had been used to mark where bodies had lain before being moved. Only later did they learn that those were the shadows of people who had been vaporized by the atomic heat.

One of the prisoners, Al Maxwell, reported that he and others very quickly developed terrible sunburns. In reality, these were beta burns, which are caused by the energy released from disintegrating atoms. To rest, the men lay down in the powdery gray dust that blanketed the city. They soon developed a rash, and in Al Maxwell's case it lasted until his death forty years later.

A month later, victorious U.S. military personnel arrived in the ruins of those Japanese cities. The atomic events and terrible toll in human lives were of more than human and historical interest. They were also of scientific and medical interest, for never before had so many people been exposed to such a massive dose of radiation. Nuclear scientists knew of the danger in a few individual instances. Marie Curie, for example, had died of leukemia years after discovering and working with radium. Scientists knew that radiation could kill, but they had little information about how well the human organism could tolerate it, how health could be protected, and how different isotopes and types of radiation affected different organs, tissue, cells, and the immune system. Although the atomic annihilations in Japan would remain in the world's conscience as an illustration of how horrific war can be, the two sites also served as nuclear laboratories.

Before American troops were sent into Hiroshima and Nagasaki, General Groves sent in a medical team to measure levels of radiation, and in the words of General Groves's deputy, General Thomas Farrell, to prove that there was no radioactivity from the bomb.[2] The team succeeded in that mission. Quick two-day surveys of both cities found no traces of radioactivity in the ground, streets, ashes, or other materials. A more careful survey conducted over the next few weeks determined higher levels at hypocenter, the area directly below the point where the bomb exploded. The levels were considered safe, however.

In retrospect, these findings are quite surprising, if not downright dubious. The bombs had to have released quite a bit of radiation. Failure to detect radiation had several causes. One was that the radiation detectors used were relatively crude; readings could have been off by 30 percent. Also, the team may have been encouraged to not find radiation and may not have been properly trained to find it. Most of the members were doctors, not nuclear scientists. Also, no one knew what level of radioactivity was unsafe. The level that is considered unsafe has been dropping steadily since that time. Continued research, including ongoing surveys of bombing victims, has found that even very low doses are harmful to at least some people.

U.S. marines and Navy seabees arrived in Hiroshima and Nagasaki on September 8, after the area had been declared safe. Humans would not be allowed to enter such a highly radioactive area today, and it is uncertain whether authorities knew of the possibility of danger. Apparently the authorities were surprised at the level of radiation, which was far higher than had first been reported. Nonetheless, the marines were allowed to work and live in the area without wearing protective face masks or special clothing. They drank contaminated water from the local reservoir, ate local contaminated food, and used brooms to dust fallout from their clothing.[3] (Under today's standards, no one would even attempt to decontaminate such clothes. They would be placed in special containers and buried as radioactive waste.)

Even though medical specialists immediately began studies of the local population to determine the effects of radiation, no one similarly checked American military personnel. Such a study could have helped scientists understand the effects of the radiation that would later spread across North America following atomic bomb tests. If doctors had tracked the health of these first atomic soldiers, the information would have expanded medical knowledge considerably. It also would have made it easier for the veterans to claim benefits to which they, as soldiers wounded in active duty, were entitled.

Massive nuclear tragedies have been rare in history. Since the linkage of radiation to health is determined by statistics, massive nuclear tragedies are opportunities for radiologists to gather invaluable information. Unfortunately, the U.S. government did not take full advantage of the tragic opportunities at Hiroshima and Nagasaki and locations downwind from the Nevada Test Site. Instead, the government denied that any dangers existed. The consistent message from the government was that the radiation was too low to cause any harmful effects. It was never considered a matter that called for study.

OPERATION CROSSROADS: THE MARSHALL ISLAND, 1946

At the end of World War II, for a too brief moment in history, the world seemed stable and at peace. Germany and Japan, aggressors in a global war, had been soundly defeated. The United States dominated the world and had exclusive possession of atomic power.

On August 1, 1946, President Truman signed the Atomic Energy Act, creating the Atomic Energy Commission, a federal agency charged with overseeing the civilian and military uses of nuclear power. Its board of directors, five civilian commissioners and a general manager, were to be appointed by the president and approved by the Senate in order to have civilians control atomic weapons. The first five general managers, it turned out, were military men, and one of the first commissioners, Lewis Strauss, was an admiral in the Naval Reserve. Seventy percent of the AEC budget over the next fifteen years would be dedicated to weapons development.[4]

General Groves wanted to immediately test three more bombs. The military needed to know not only how effective such weapons could be against an enemy but how friendly forces could defend themselves against the explosion and radiation. The Navy was especially interested in research into how well atomic bombs would work as weapons against naval fleets.

For these first tests, old U.S. ships and Japanese and German warships captured in the war were loaded with such typical military equipment as trucks, weapons, ammunition, fuel, and general gear. The ships also carried live animals; all together there were 200 goats, 200 pigs, and 5,000 mice and guinea pigs.

This initial test series, code-named Crossroads, detonated three devices in the summer of 1946, less than a year after the end of the war. The test shots were called Able, Baker, and Charlie. Able exploded at 900 feet (about 275 m) above the fleet. Once results were gathered and tallied, Baker was detonated 180 feet (55 m) below the surface of the water. Charlie was to explode deep under the sea.

A joint task force of Army and Navy personnel was formed to conduct the tests. The Manhattan District was responsible for safety. The task force found an ideal test site: the Bikini Atoll in the Marshall Islands, a U.S. trust territory. This trusteeship had been granted by the United Nations. While it didn't make the Marshall Islands a U.S. territory, it gave the United States the right to serve as the government and to do as it pleased there, including remove residents from their homes and bombard their islands with atomic weapons.

As a test site, Bikini Atoll was perfect. A ring of islands offered a calm harbor for the anchoring of 173 target ships and 200 operations ships. The weather tended to be calm and predictable. The only problem was that people lived there.

People can be moved, however, and the U.S. government explained to the 162 Bikinians who lived there that the tests were necessary to ensure that atomic weapons could be used for the good of all mankind and to end war on earth. They described in detail the power of the bombs. The Bikinians, a religious people willing to do what they could for mankind (and not willing to argue with anyone armed with the weapons so clearly described) accepted temporary resettlement on the island of Rongerik, some 130 miles (210 km) away.

They believed that they could move back as soon as the tests were over.

The dangers of the shock wave, light, and heat were already known. A more important concern was the spread and effect of radiation. The effect of the Able air burst was relatively predictable. It would be the fourth air burst since the Trinity test. Scientists already knew approximately how much radiation would be produced and how far it would go under certain weather conditions.

The Baker test was harder to predict. An explosion underwater, the world's first, would irradiate the water, making it radioactive, and that water would be vaporized and heaved high into the air. The fission products produced by the chain reaction, and the fuel not consumed by the chain reaction, would remain concentrated in the water. A pretest report predicted that the water near a recent surface explosion would be a witch's brew—probably enough plutonium near the surface of the water to poison the entire combined armed forces of the United States at their highest wartime strength. The fission products would be worse. Another task force document predicted that the lagoon and largest ships would undoubtedly not be habitable until some weeks after the underwater shot. [5]

Much of the radiation in the air fell as rain, called rainout, as had happened at Hiroshima and Nagasaki. Rainout is extremely radioactive. It brings down airborne radionuclides—the radioactive atoms— before they thin out in the wind.

Shot Able, detonated on July 1, 1946, went well. Ships that survived the blast picked up little radiation. Shot Baker, detonated on July 25, proved much more difficult and dangerous. The explosion near the bottom of the lagoon heaved up a half-mile- (0.8-km-) wide column of water, all of it instantly radioactive. Much of it came down as rain, soaking the target ships and surrounding area for about an hour. A dense mist wafted across the lagoon, the most poisonous cloud that ever existed in the history of the world, contaminating the ships inside and out.[6] Radiation specialists had hoped to at least board the target ships to measure the effects before much radiation burned off by breaking down into nonradioactive isotopes. They had to hold off, however. Only the ships upwind were safe to board and then only for a while. The Crossroads technical director, Ralph Sawyer, said the radiation created by the explosion was roughly equivalent to that from several thousand tons of radium.[7] (A few millionths of a gram of radium lodged in the human body has proven to be deadly.) An hour after the explosion, some ships closest to the target were emitting radiation at a rate of 1,200 roentgens per day, three times the lethal dose. The daily allowable dose would have been reached in three seconds.[8]

The 20 experimental pigs and 200 rats in the inner rooms, therefore, were doomed. All the pigs and a third of the rats died within a month, and the rest died within the next two months. They had received doses of 310 to 2700 roentgens, enough to kill humans either by radiation poisoning or, eventually, by cancer.

Contamination spread to the task force operations fleet. Men returning from target ships brought radiation onboard. It also came in through water ducts that used seawater. It attached itself to hulls in the form of radioactive algae and barnacles. Later tests would show that some marine organisms can concentrate enough radionuclides to emit radioactivity 100,000 times the background level.[9] Several sleeping quarters against the hull or salt water pipes had to be abandoned. Scraping algae off the hulls helped, but not much. Water filters were ineffective. Eventually a separate ship had to be reserved just for laundry operations where clean-up crews could leave their radioactive clothes, and eventually that ship had to be abandoned, too.

Within two weeks after the shot, the chief medical adviser of the task force recommended calling off all further work in the area. The target ships were hopelessly contaminated, he said, and the risk to workers was too high. Higher officials did not agree, but they did move the fleet farther away from the lagoon. After considerable protests by the medical adviser, it was decided that most of the fleet could return to Pearl Harbor, Hawaii, on August 10. A month later, President Truman announced that the third shot, Charlie, which was to have been detonated under deep water, was canceled.

TREACHEROUS TIMES

The American monopoly on nuclear power would not last long. The Soviet Union, defender of the communist way of life, was determined not to let itself be weaker than any foreign power.[10] Although General Groves had predicted that the supposedly underdeveloped Soviet Union would take twenty years to build an atomic weapon, on August 29, 1949, it revealed its membership in the nuclear club with the explosion of an atomic bomb in Siberia.[11] The western world found out by detecting the radiation as it blew out of Asia.

It was immediately clear that the United States and the Soviet Union were in a race to lead the world in nuclear power. The fear on both sides was that if either country let the other get ahead, the more powerful country might be tempted to eradicate the other. Unfortunately, progress in the new science of atomic weaponry called for a lot of experimentation.

When, in 1948, Czechoslovakia fell to a Soviet-inspired communist takeover and communist East Germany blockaded West Germany's side of Berlin, the spread of communism looked ominous. In 1949, Mao Zedong's communist forces took over China, putting most of Asia's population under communist control. When communist North Korea invaded noncommunist South Korea in 1950, the communist bloc's intentions of global expansion seemed clear.

The United States officials worried about communist agents and spies working within the U.S. government. In the early 1950s, Senator Joseph McCarthy of Wisconsin began what was later called a witch-hunt for alleged communists. With little or no evidence, Senator McCarthy accused not only specific government employees but also college professors, artists, writers, scientists, actors, and others of being communists. Many of them lost their jobs because of nothing more than the accusation and a general fear that bordered on paranoia that communism was out to take over the world, and it was increasingly apparent that the Soviet Union had an atomic arsenal that could do it. Nuclear war began to look inevitable.

With this external threat and internal fear, the United States government felt justified in testing atomic weapons as often as it considered necessary. The presumable alternative, Soviet atomic bombs exploding over American cities, seemed incalculably worse than the explosion of American atomic bombs in test sites in the desert of Nevada and the atolls of the Marshall Islands. The American nuclear arsenal may well have been all that warded off a Soviet attack. The painful irony is that America's nuclear test program came to look too much like a nuclear war against the United States itself.

T H R E E

TESTING IN NEVADA 1951–1958

The Atomic Energy Commission was given the power to regulate everything atomic, from nuclear power plants to atomic bomb tests to bomb production to waste disposal. It also supervised itself and determined which of its activities would remain secret and whether any of its activities were dangerous. Certainly much of this secrecy was necessary in the tense times of the early nuclear arms race. Over the next two decades, however, when the AEC faced criticism, it often hid information that had little to do with national security but much to do with public safety.

THE NEVADA TESTS

Atomic testing had started in the Marshall Islands because President Truman had considered such explosions too dangerous to take place on American soil. In 1949 the commissioner of the AEC, Sumner Pike, declared that only a national emergency could justify testing in the United States. As tension increased between the United States, the Soviet Union, and China, and the war in Korea heated up, President Truman directed the AEC to find a site more accessible to military and scientific personnel, more secure from foreign observation, and more quickly reachable.

The Nevada Test Site (NTS) was chosen for a few relatively low-order detonations.[1] Until the Army transferred ownership of the NTS to the AEC, the property had been known as the Tonopah Gunnery Range. It was called the Nevada Proving Grounds until 1957. Its desolate 1,350 square miles (about 3,500 sq km) of desert lay in a broad, flat area bordered on the north by high ridges. Las Vegas was about 60 miles (about 100 km) to the southeast. The weather was predictable, and the lack of rain would minimize concentrations of fallout. The prevailing winds blew east, away from the densely populated coast of California. No one lived within a radius of several miles, and the nearest urban area was considered, in the words of an AEC memo, a low-use segment of the population.[2] When another AEC document called the area virtually uninhabited, the people who lived there responded wryly by calling themselves "virtual uninhabitants."[3] A hundred thousand of them "uninhabited" the areas downwind of the test site. They also became known as "downwinders."

The AEC also considered using Amchitka Island, off the coast of Alaska, as a site for at least the more dangerous tests, but it would have been more difficult to follow radioactive clouds as they drifted over. In Nevada, the clouds could be tracked by scientists in jeeps.[4]

One objective of the tests was to develop tactical nuclear weapons that could be used on a battlefield rather than over a city. AEC commissioner Gordon Dean specifically stated that they hoped to develop a nuclear arsenal that paralleled the conventional arsenal, including nuclear artillery shells, torpedoes, rockets, guided missiles, mines, and bombs for small battlefield bombers.

Was the AEC aware that the tests might endanger local people? Apparently so. In a memo dated May 22, 1951, reporting on a meeting to discuss the safety of upcoming tests, Shields Warren, director of the AEC Division of Biology and Medicine, warned, "I would almost say from the discussion thus far that in the light of the size and activity of some of these [radioactive] particles, their unpredictability, the possibility of external beta burns, is quite real." A civilian scientist at the meeting countered, "The time has come when we should take some risk and get some information for the future situation. In other words, we are faced with a war in which atomic weapons will undoubtedly be used, and we have to have some information about these things."[5]

The committee agreed that the threat of atomic war was more serious than possible off-site injuries. The tests had to happen *somewhere.* The Soviet Union was testing constantly and was keeping up with the United States, megaton for megaton. In May 9, 1951, the United States tested its first hydrogen bomb in the Marshall Islands. In July, the Soviet Union tested its first hydrogen bomb. The nuclear arms race was growing in several directions. Both sides wanted to have not only the biggest bomb but also the smallest, that is, tactical weapons that could be used without endangering nearby friendly forces. Each side wanted a clean bomb that would produce relatively little fallout. They wanted to know how many kilotons they could explode on the other side of the world without endangering home territory with fallout. They had to study fallout patterns, triggering devices, detonator designs, fuels, and the effects on nearby civilians, troops, equipment, and buildings. None of this was possible without detonating experimental weapons, and the side that didn't experiment was going to fall behind in the race. To fall behind, to become weaker, might be to practically ask for attack.

Failure to improve nuclear weapons through testing could very well lead to nuclear war. NTS manager Thomas Clark has stated that the testing program was the main reason why nuclear war never occurred.[6]

Each test gave scientists the information they needed to move on to the next stage of weapons development. The urgency often meant sticking to a schedule even if it compromised safety. Test managers, who had responsibility for each test, were under considerable pressure to stay on schedule. Tests were conducted under less than ideal weather conditions that sent fallout toward populated areas.[7]

The first tests in Nevada began with Operation Ranger in January and February 1951. Preshot planners had real concerns for off-site safety. Calculations predicted that 25-kiloton bombs could be exploded above the ground without exceeding the allowed dose of 6 to 12 roentgens beyond a 100-mile (161-km) radius. Monitors in cars, trucks, and airplanes would track the drift of fallout. Two weeks before the first test, residents were warned there would be periodic blasts in the near future, but there would be no announcement of upcoming test times.[8]

The first blast was seen and heard as far away as San Diego and Los Angeles, not to mention in such nearby communities as Las Vegas, Nevada, and St. George, Utah. By the fifth blast, local residents considered the flash and tremor an almost natural occurrence.

Subsequent shots tested all sorts of warheads, triggering devices, delivery systems, and fallout effects. Shot Able, the first test in Operation Buster-Jangle, was fired atop a 100-foot (30-m) tower. It fizzled, yielding under 0.1 kiloton. In 1953 Simon was detonated atop a 300-foot (about 90-m) tower just 2,000 yards (about 1,800 m) from troops in trenches. Shot Grable, fired from an artillery cannon 7 miles (11 km) away, exploded over trees, buildings, bomb shelters, and vehicles that had been set up to test the bomb's effect. Operation Plumbob tested warheads carried by balloons, towers, and air-to-air missiles and also experimented with the results of warheads triggered by a plane crash or other accident.

SHOT HARRY'S RADIOACTIVE CLOUD

One particularly serious incident happened on a May day in 1953 when Shot Harry was detonated on a 300-foot (90-m) tower. The 32-kiloton explosion heaved a vast amount of vaporized earth into the air, most of it as a fine powder and all of it radioactive. The particles came to earth in a relatively small area, exposing the lower half of Utah to intense radiation rather than exposing a broad swath of North America to relatively diluted radiation. Many people suspect that that particular shot, if not all shots, was a fallout experiment. The citizens of St. George were not warned even when the shot managers knew in which direction the cloud was going.

Two Utah state health officials were driving to a uranium mine north of St. George when their car was swamped in dense black cloud. With visibility at zero, they stopped, got out and ran in fear of oncoming traffic. Minutes later, three other cars collided nearby, and one hit their car. When they used their Geiger counter to take a reading, the needle went to the end of the scale, indicating a level above 100 roentgens per hour, more than a person should be exposed to in over twenty years.

JoAnn Taylor, a college student, drove into the same cloud of radiation, which came down on her car as rain, though the AEC denied that it had rained anywhere within a thousand miles (about 1,600 km) downwind of the test. Frank Butrico, the radiation monitor assigned to St. George, took a reading of Taylor's car when she arrived in St. George, then directed her to the nearest car wash, where she got into a long line of radioactive cars. Local people, unaware of any problem with radiation, were being irradiated as they stood near the cars.

As the dark cloud was passing directly over St. George, Frank Butrico decided that it would be a good idea to warn the local population to stay indoors. Even though it wasn't really his job, he reported the problem to the mayor, who ordered the nearest radio station, 50 miles (80 km) away in Cedar City, to announce the danger and recommend that everyone stay indoors. By that time, however, the level of radiation had already passed its peak. Many people did not hear the announcement, and many others did not really understand the danger since it sounded no more important than a weather report. People outside of St. George, mostly farmers who worked outdoors, weren't sure if the warning applied to them.

An elementary school got the word and kept children in during morning recess; however, Butrico saw children playing outside before the danger had fully passed.

Agatha Mannering was outdoors working in her garden, not indoors listening to the radio. The fallout burned her skin where it was exposed whenever she leaned over to pull weeds. Soon her hair fell out, and she felt sick all the time. Years later, when she broke her arm, the doctor said she had the porous, brittle bones of an old woman.

Elma Mackelprang left her kids in her pickup truck while she got out to give water to her sheep. Later, she came down with a fever, diarrhea, and nausea, and then her hair and fingernails fell out. Her children in the truck suffered no symptoms. The AEC told her the problems were caused by her recent hysterectomy.

AEC officials who hurried to a uranium mine east of St. George found all the miners vomiting and covered with a sudden rash. Their official report blamed a gastrointestinal bug and possible stress after hearing the warnings on the radio.

Residents also reported an odd metallic taste in the air as the dark cloud passed overhead. Apparently they were tasting the vaporized remains of the steel tower on which the bomb had detonated.

Frank Butrico, probably the only person in town who understood anything about radiation, was also the only person who took appropriate protective measures. He stayed indoors as much as he could, and then, getting high radiation readings from his own hair, bought new clothes, took a long shower, and threw his contaminated clothes away. He didn't advise anyone else in town to do the same. It wasn't his job to do so.

A few years later, Dr. Harold Knapp, an AEC fallout specialist, calculated that levels of radioactive iodine-131 in milk had soared during the days after the test. A child drinking a liter per day would have received a dose of 120 to 440 rads to the thyroid, an extremely dangerous amount. Dr. Charles Mays, of the University of Utah, calculated that 700 infants in St. George had received doses to the thyroid that were 136 to 500 times higher than normal.

Utah newspapers reported the illnesses that followed Shot Harry along with the AEC denials of any possible connection to radiation. An editorial in Salt Lake City's *Desert News* complained that "the public is never told just what levels of radiation are reached in this area, except that the AEC reassures us that they have been well within the limits of safety."[9] Another editorial in that paper suggested that civil defense maneuvers be conducted whenever fallout passed over a given city, thus helping to protect the population while also preparing them for what to do in case of war. The AEC never acted on the suggestion, however. Communities were rarely advised of upcoming tests, were never advised of fallout until after it had arrived, were never told what levels they were exposed to, and were never honestly informed of how dangerous certain levels were.

The possibility of warning people and even evacuating them was discussed at AEC meetings before the Ranger series in 1951. In a memorandum to a safety committee, Dr. Shields Warren, director of the AEC Division of Biology and Medicine, said, "I would almost say from the discussion thus far that in the light of the size and activity of some of these particles, and their unpredictability of fallout, the possibility of external beta burns is quite real."[10] That committee decided to go ahead and take the risk because the information gained would be worth the injuries and the possible public outcry.

There was also discussion on evacuating everyone within a 44-mile (71-km) radius of ground zero, but the idea was rejected for fear of causing public panic. The AEC did not want to incite protest by revealing possible dangers. It was more important that the public have confidence in its government and the safety of atomic explosions in their country. On the same day that President Truman approved the Nevada Test Site, members of the AEC met to plan not safety but the higher priority issue of public relations. The talks focused on the questions of exploring radiological safety aspects in order to make the public feel at home with atomic blasts and radiation hazards.[11] Years later, a Public Health Service radiation monitor reflected the cynicism of the time when he said, "You can't underestimate the importance of public relations when you are trying to dump radioactive material on people, and we stressed it continually."[12]

The AEC's efforts to protect the public from fallout

were limited to public relations and education. The public relations aspect aimed at convincing people that there was no danger, and the education effort minimized the danger and the need for protective measures. Despite many reports from uranium prospectors whose Geiger counters detected radiation above 100 roentgens, the AEC claimed that exposures could be measured only in thousandths of roentgens and maintained that the off-site levels of radiation were not harmful. Although scientific knowledge showed that radiation was most harmful when particles entered the body, AEC educational materials never suggested that garden crops, meat, and dairy products should be destroyed if exposed to fallout. Although AEC officials knew enough to discard contaminated clothes and thoroughly wash the body and hair after exposure, citizens were merely advised to dust off their clothes, wash their hands, and bathe more often.[13] To allay public suspicion and anxiety, the chairman of the AEC Military Liaison Committee discouraged such measures as setting up roadblocks and washing the stopped cars, which he described as the kind of overreaction that caused public concern.[14]

Meanwhile, strange things continued to happen to the "virtual inhabitants" of the vicinity of the NTS. Martha Laird of Twin Springs, Nevada, remembered the ground shaking and rumbling like an earthquake, and that the shock wave blew their front door off. Ena Cooper of Indian Springs, Nevada, says gravel on the ground danced a foot (30 cm) in the air. Jamie Stewart, a little girl at the time, saw ashes fall like snow, and when she shook trees, the big, gray flakes showered down on her. Claudia Peterson, also a child at the time, remembers the big fireball that rose in the distance and the cloud that passed overhead and that men came into her classroom with Geiger counters. She remembers big piles of dead lambs on her father's farm. Marjorie Black found twelve dead cows and several dead rabbits and magpies in her pasture. Once, when snow melted off her truck, all the paint peeled off. LaVerl Snyder was camping when she saw clouds boil over her campsite. A rash broke out over her body, and then her skin burned and blistered. Over the next several days she felt nauseous. Then her toenails and fingernails fell off. Then her hair fell out. At the hospital, doctors diagnosed her problem as "sunstroke."

This "low-use segment of the population" included 10,000 people in Utah's Washington County, 140 miles (225 km) east of the test site. In the rare cases when they were warned of an upcoming blast, people in St. George opened their doors and windows to lessen the effects of the shock wave. Often plate-glass windows popped out of their frames. Sometimes the AEC set up roadblocks to prevent cars from leaving town in the direction of a passing cloud. Incoming cars were directed to the nearest car wash. Occasionally an announcement on the radio would suggest that people stay indoors, but the announcements often came only after the cloud had arrived.[15] Homeowners were advised to hose down their roofs. People generally assumed that fallout was like snow flurries, that it melted away after a few hours.

It would have helped a lot if people had stayed indoors for a few hours after fallout passed. The radioactive strength of the fallout declined rapidly with time. Even when there were warnings, they were heard only by people who were already indoors and listening to the radio. Many people in this agricultural community were outdoors all day and never knew about the invisible danger showering down from the sky.

Years later, in a court case concerning AEC negligence, Frank Butrico explained the reasons for the secrecy. He testified that senior officials had told him that the AEC was going to stop disseminating informa-tion. "Let's cool it," they said, as Butrico reported it. "Let's try to get this thing quieted down a little bit because if we don't, then it's likely that there might be some suggestion made for curtailing the test program. And this, in the interest of our national defense, we can-not do."[16]

RADIATION ACROSS AMERICA

Radioactive fallout was not restricted to the vicinity around the NTS site or even to the surrounding states. Here and there across the continent, rain and wind focused enough fallout to create hot spots. One such hot spot was Rensselaer Polytechnic Institute (RPI) in Troy, New York. One morning after a heavy rainstorm, RPI physics students happened to have Geiger counters working. They found radiation—from Shot Simon—everywhere, indoors and out. An average of 16 million atoms was disintegrating each second in each square foot of the campus, and each of those disintegrations released a bit of radioactivity. That morning, RPI was more radioactive than some places at the NTS.[17] Years later, Dr. Ernest Sternglass studied the rates of thyroid cancer, leukemia, and infant mortality in the Troy area and found all those rates above normal.[18]

In 1955, the most intense series to date, Operation Teapot, was to detonate twelve devices, some of them rather large. Foreseeing public distress, the AEC beefed up its public relations campaign. It decided that infor-mation given to the public should distinguish between bombs of over 30 kilotons and bombs that were small-er—and by implication less harmful. An AEC document said, "The goal should be to describe the larger tests as unpleasant but necessary . . . limited to the smallest number possible. . . [with] small-yield tests as completely controlled experiments [that] will not affect the public . . . and will have as their purpose the development of atomic warheads [that] would be used over our own cities to protect against enemy air attack." In short, all tests would be sold as "friendly blasts" offering comforting protection.[19]

In January 1955, the AEC held a secret meeting to discuss its Project Sunshine to collect parts of human bodies from around the world to check them for signs of fallout. At the meeting, Dr. Willard Libby, a researcher who later won the Nobel Prize in chemistry, told the commission that there were great gaps in data about fallout because researchers didn't have samples of human tissue, especially from children. He wanted to look for signs of strontium-90, which, being chemically similar to calcium, readily attaches to bones. "Human samples are of prime importance," he told the AEC, "and if anybody knows how to do a good job of body snatching, they will really be serving their country." Eventually, more than 1,500 samples were collected from various countries. Researchers at Columbia University reported that no significant amounts of strontium-90 were found in humans worldwide.[20]

UNDERGROUND TESTING

On October 31, 1958, the United States, Soviet Union, and England, by mutual agreement, ceased all testing of nuclear weapons. Only France continued. When the Soviet Union announced three years later that it would resume testing, AEC chairman Glenn T. Seaborg recommended that the United States refrain from resuming tests. After the Soviets exploded a monster 50-megaton device, however, President John Kennedy gave the order for a U.S. resumption of testing. U.S. tests, however, except for one, would be underground to prevent fallout from escaping into the atmosphere.

The intentions were better than the results. Atomic explosives were implanted in vertical shafts anywhere from 100 feet (30 m) to several thousand feet deep. Tests were also conducted in tunnels that ran deep into the sides of mountains. The efforts at containing radiation underground were far from successful. From 1961 to 1964, almost half of 142 announced tests leaked radiation into the atmosphere.[21] Operation Hardtack II, conducted in 1958, included four weapons tests, of which only one did not vent radioactivity into the atmosphere. The first shot in 1961, a 2.6-kiloton explosion in a tunnel that went 4,000 feet (1.2 km) into Rainier Mesa, was followed by a radioactive steam explosion fifteen minutes later. Soon, highly radioactive water was leaking from the mouth of the tunnel. A month later, another tunnel shot released a cloud of radioactivity, and six months later, Shot Platte released a dark cloud that swept over the testing site from four locations. Fallout exceeded acceptable levels 115 miles away. Two months later, Shot Des Moines vented in three places, sending a cloud that raised radiation to dangerous levels as far as 75 miles (120 km) away.

When the AEC fired a test shot near Carlsbad, New Mexico, the local population was assured that venting of radiation was impossible. The explosion would occur 1,200 feet (365 m) below the earth's surface in a bedrock of salt to see if the salt would hold the heat. If so, it would open the possibility of using nuclear explosions to produce steam that would generate electricity.

The explosion created so much steam that a radioactive geyser broke through the ground and shot 300 feet (over 90 m) into the air. So much radiation escaped that scientists had to wait three days before they could go in to take experimental readings, and it was months before recovery operations could start.

INTERNATIONAL TESTS

As we have already seen, in the 1950s the Soviet Union was testing just as much as the United States, and the consequences to human health were probably just as bad. In the 1950s, England tested bombs in Australia and the Pacific. In the 1960s, France tested in the Algerian Sahara and, like its allies, in the Pacific. In 1964, China began testing, too.

Between 1952 and 1958, the British tested twenty-two nuclear devices. Twelve were detonated on the Australian mainland or just off the coast. Nine were tested on Christmas Island. Australian prime minister Robert Menzies, who approved the use of his country for the tests, considered it a contribution to the defense of democracy.

The contribution came with an unexpected cost, however. Aborigine natives near the tests were exposed to fallout. One tribe reported being swamped by a black mist, a fact unknown to the public until almost twenty years later. Many aborigines were allowed to live in contaminated areas.

Several nonatomic tests of fuels and components spread radioactive plutonium, uranium, and beryllium across an area of desert. The only possible cleanup measure was to plow the soil over in hope that the radioactive material would stay beneath the surface. However, most of the plutonium that was plowed under or buried in shallow pits, has come to the surface and been blown about by desert winds. Radiation levels are now 100 times more than expected, and plutonium has been found in aborigine camps 80 miles (about 130 km) from the site.[22]

The British also tested seven fusion devices and two fission devices on Christmas Island in the South Pacific. The tests of some of the largest hydrogen bombs ever detonated in the atmosphere were done quickly during the final months before the United States and the Soviet Union agreed to ban tests in the atmosphere, oceans, and outer space.

The French have tested 172 fission and fusion bombs above and below ground, nearly one test for each twenty bombs they built. The first test, in 1960, was conducted in the Sahara Desert of Algeria, which was a French colony at the time. Fallout was detected around the world. Algerian television and the news wire service Agence France Presse claimed that 150 Algerian prisoners were exposed to the blast, but the government denied the allegations.[23] Three other atmospheric tests and thirteen underground tests were conducted in Algeria.

When Algeria gained its independence, France found new test sites in the South Pacific. On the islands of Mororoa and Fangataufa, between 1966 and 1974, long after the United States and Soviet Union had stopped atmospheric tests, the French detonated forty-four bombs above ground. Islands 2,000 miles (3,200 km) to the west were contaminated. Their underground tests also continued. In 1980, a tropical storm ripped the asphalt from a nuclear-waste burial ground on Mororoa. Within four months, radiation levels on the island doubled. Trade unionists refused to work there. In 1987, five days of underwater research by Jacques Cousteau revealed no significant contamination but found huge fissures, landslides, and craters in the ocean floor, probably the result of the underground tests.[24]

Both the New Zealand government and the Greenpeace organization protested against the French tests and sent ships into the area in the 1970s to prevent further tests. In 1982, Greenpeace sent two ships around the South Pacific to protest the tests. In 1985, secret agents of the French government blew up the Greenpeace ship *Rainbow Warrior* in New Zealand's Aukland Harbour to prevent further disruptions in France's testing program.[25] In December 1995, the United Nations passed a resolution that deplored all nuclear tests and strongly urged their end. No countries were named, but France criticized its European neighbors who voted for the resolution.[26]

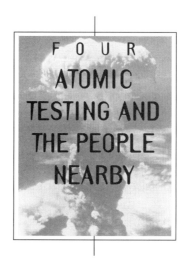

F O U R
ATOMIC TESTING AND THE PEOPLE NEARBY

The testing of atomic devices took place during a time when the United States feared atomic attack by the Soviet Union. Any American counterattack would have been atomic as well. To conduct such a war, the military needed to know how nuclear explosions would affect troops in the field.

In July of 1951, the military asked the AEC for permission to have soldiers take part in maneuvers that would simulate atomic warfare. The request came just after the first series of tests, Operation Ranger held in Nevada. The original proposal was to have 5,000 troops take up combat positions at a barely safe distance from a test detonation, then advance into the affected area. The chairman of the AEC readily agreed, provided that the military would accept responsibility for the safety and living conditions of the troops.[1]

The military had two objectives for carrying out the tests: to train the troops to operate during an atomic attack, and to assess their psychological response to a nearby atomic explosion. Documents that were top secret for many years revealed no serious intentions of testing the long-term effects of radiation, which apparently were not of concern.

With the approval of the AEC, the Army constructed Camp Desert Rock at the Nevada Test Site. The soldiers assigned to the camp were given booklets that explained the importance of secrecy. They were prohibited from talking about the tests, the military maneuvers, or any effects they felt from the tests. Ironically, they were warned about the dangers of poisonous snakes and insects, but the more deadly danger of radiation was not mentioned. A training film said that radiation was the least important effect and that it was fatal only within a mile (1.6 km) of the explosion. The men were taught that they could survive an atomic attack and live to fight another day, and that this explosion was one of the most beautiful sights ever seen by man.[2]

To establish a realistic scenario for the experimental maneuvers, an imaginary war was created for Operation Buster-Jangle, the second series in Nevada. A hypothetical aggressor enemy using tactics and formations common among communist armies, had invaded the northwest of the United States. The U.S. army had retreated to a battle line that reached from Los Angeles to Las Vegas. Here the American forces would hold the line. To counterattack, they would have to use tactical atomic weapons. As soon as the bombs detonated, U.S. troops would charge into the hole that had been blown open in the aggressor's lines.

The American forces were to dig into trenches and foxholes a safe distance from ground zero. Following the detonation, they would march forward. One purpose was to simply assess the physical effects: how well the men stood up to the shock wave, how effectively trenches sheltered them, and how much the radiation would affect their ability to fight.

The maneuvers would also train the soldiers to operate under those conditions. Most of that training was psychological. An atomic battleground is a frightening place, especially to anyone who has doesn't know what to expect. A single experience would prepare a soldier for the blinding white flash of light, the powerful, earth-jolting shock wave, the scorching heat, the debilitating radiation, and the general scene of fire, smoke, and destruction.

The first Buster-Jangle test was of a very small tactical bomb with a 0.1 kiloton yield. The most powerful detonation involving soldiers yielded 31 kilotons, two and a half times more powerful than the Hiroshima bomb. Almost 3,000 troops observed explosions in the Operation Buster-Jangle series. Still, they stayed more than six miles (about 10 km) from the detonation, as required under AEC policy, and radiation experts monitored conditions as the troops advanced.

That experiment went well, too well to simulate realistic war conditions. Military leaders decided that, to be effective, maneuvers would have to come closer to the real thing. The soldiers would have to be close enough to feel fear and to suffer at least some negative effects. In a real war the troops would not be preceded by radiation monitors telling them where to go and when to stop.

The AEC protested. Dr. Shields Warren, the AEC medical officer, recommended that soldiers not be exposed to increased danger because if some were injured or killed, it would be bad public relations. He also might have been against the experiment for humanitarian reasons. He officially stated that each test is experimental and its yield cannot be predicted with accuracy.[3]

But the military insisted, and the Department of Defense agreed to accept all responsibility for safety and injuries. The AEC backed down, and in the next series of tests, troops were assigned to foxholes just 7,000 yards (about 4 miles or 6 km) from ground zero. Soon the maximum permissible dose for soldiers was doubled from 3 to 6 rad, as measured, quite inaccurately, by exposure badges. Tanks, jeeps, rifles, artillery, ammunition, and other equipment were deployed to see what the explosion would do to them. Cattle were tied to stakes at various distances, and smaller animals were locked in cages.

The men knew nothing about the dangers they faced. They were told that the radiation levels would be minimal and perfectly safe. They were not informed of even the most basic protective measures. Their health was not monitored after the tests, and they were never advised to watch for symptoms of the illnesses caused by radiation. Years later, when the illnesses began to occur, the military and AEC denied responsibility and the Veterans Administration denied them benefits. At the time of the tests, the soldiers were warned never to reveal that they had witnessed an atomic explosion.

Most of the soldiers were boys in their teens or early twenties, young enough to still feel themselves immortal. Machismo, or at least a fear of being seen as scared, led them to downplay their concern. Some men were ordered to take positions a few miles from ground zero. Others, in later tests, volunteered to take forward positions just a few thousand yards from the explosion.

The men were told to kneel in their trenches, put their backs against the wall closest to ground zero, and cover their eyes until after the initial flash of light. Some, though by no means all, of the men wore exposure badges to measure gamma radiation, but there were no attempts to measure exposure to internal or external beta or alpha radiation.

An hour after the 31-kiloton explosion of Shot Charlie, the troops were trucked into the area where the equipment was deployed. Half an hour later, paratroopers were dropped in. Some of the soldiers walked within 175 yards (160 m) of ground zero, where the radiation was probably over 100 roentgens. Things seemed to go well. The observable effects of radiation—no one had any idea what would happen twenty years later—were minimal and temporary.

In the next series of tests, Operation Upshot-Knothole, troops were moved in closer. Some officers who were given a little training in the nature of nuclear explosions were allowed to calculate how close they could go. They had to fill out a form attesting that they had been trained and were volunteering to witness the blast at a distance of their choosing. A trench was prepared just 2,500 yards (1.4 miles or 2.3 km) from ground zero, which nine officers manned and in which they survived the explosion. Three thousand troops took shelter further back, then charged to within half a mile (0.8 km) of the explosion.

A month later, Shot Badger involved almost 3,000 participants, who were either deployed in trenches 2.3 miles (3.7 km) from ground zero or were quickly brought in by helicopter after the explosion. Animals were tied even closer. Radiation in the trench exceeded the 500-roentgen-per-hour limit of the radiation measuring equipment. A thousand yards (over 900 m) from ground zero, where the troops were inspecting test target equipment, readings showed 50 roentgens per hour.[4]

Robert Carter, seventeen years old at the time, was among those who witnessed Shot Hood. At 74 kilotons, it was the largest atmospheric nuclear explosion to occur within the United States. Although supposedly a fission bomb, an official at the Defense Nuclear Agency has alleged that it was actually a prototype of a new hydrogen bomb.[5] The bomb hung from a balloon in the sky. The explosion threw Carter and the men with him 40 feet (12 m) into the side of a mountain. He describes the ground as being so hot he could hardly stand on it. He felt as though he was being cooked as the vast fireball rose above them. The men then had to make their way toward ground zero, which, up close, was radiating 500 to 1,000 roentgens per hour. Along the way they saw animals that had burned to death in cages. Carter also swears he saw men, alive, inside a chain-link cage. They were wearing denim pants but no shirts. Their skin was peeling and their hair was falling out. Other soldiers in his platoon reported the same thing, and their testimonies later appeared in a legal brief in the *Washington Law Review*.[6] There is no other evidence to support his claim, however.

Carter was very ill on the way back to camp. He had a bad sunburn from beta particles, and he was nauseated, dizzy, and disoriented. A doctor told him he was suffering from radiation illness. Later, his hair fell out in clumps and his health grew worse. When he told a doctor that he had seen live humans in a cage at the test site, he was sent to a psychiatric hospital in Colorado. There he was accused of treason for what he had said and was warned not to repeat his story elsewhere. He was terrified by the experience, which he described as brainwashing. Today he is confined to a wheelchair and has been diagnosed as clinically paranoid.[7]

Robert Merron, nineteen years old, witnessed the same explosion from a trench just 3,000 feet (more than 900 m) away. He and everyone around him wept uncontrollably as the fireball rose directly above them, searing them as if they were at the door of a furnace. Mannequins above the trench burst into flames. After the men dug themselves out of the collapsed trench, they saw a hellish landscape of blackened sand and burning bushes. They were given gas masks before being ordered to march into ground zero. Merron had had 6 feet (almost 2 m) of his intestines removed by the time he was thirty. Then he had a fibroid the size of an orange removed from his gut, and he now has two fused disks in his back.

Many records of military personnel have disappeared, and those that still exist state that almost none of the military personnel received an excessive dose of radiation. There is a strong possibility that records showing the actual, higher readings are being kept secret. In 1982, a former Army medic, Van R. Brandon, said that he had been ordered to keep two sets of books during the tests. One set was to show that no one received an exposure above the approved dosimeter reading, he said. The other set of books was to show what the actual reading was. That set of books was brought in a locked briefcase attached to an officer's wrist by a set of handcuffs every morning.[8] In the absence of records, veterans could not receive medical disability compensation years later when they came down with many illnesses.

THE NEVADA TEST SITE'S NEIGHBORS

The Nevada Test Site, although in a desert, was not far from human communities. The surrounding area was dotted by ranches. To the east, in the usual path of the wind that crossed the site, lay several small cities and towns in Utah. The closest of these was St. George, 135 miles (about 215 km) away, with a population of about 5,000. Las Vegas was only 70 miles (113 km) to the south, but the winds rarely carried fallout in that direction. In all, some 100,000 people lived within the range of heavy fallout.[9] Tourist brochures often called that area the Land of Color. *U.S. News and World Report,* however, dubbed St. George "Fallout City."[10]

The majority of the people in Utah and rural Nevada, and 90 percent of St. George, were Mormons. Obeying the strict lifestyle guidelines of their religion, they avoided the use of alcohol, tobacco, and caffeine, three known causes of cancer. These people were descendants of pioneers and proud of their self-sufficiency. During the 1950s, 55 percent of the people of southwestern Utah drank milk from their own cows, and about that many drew their water from a spring. Almost half of all homes had children, and most women breast-fed their babies. Sixty-five percent ate leafy vegetables from their own gardens. Industrial pollution was very scarce in the region. Ironically, their healthy lifestyles worked against the inhabitants. The consumption of local food, water, and milk increased their intake of radioactive isotopes that cause cancer and immunological problems. Perhaps if they had eaten frozen vegetables from California, dried milk from Wisconsin, and canned food from New Jersey, they would have been better off.

NTS WORKERS

More than 200,000 civilians were contracted to work at the Nevada Test Site.[11] Some had the job of racing into the ground zero area to recover equipment that had to be assessed immediately after the detonation. In many cases, they received higher doses than soldiers or nearby residents. Many of them witnessed several tests. Unlike the soldiers, many of them worked at the NTS for several years, gradually accumulating doses. In some cases, their wives came down with cancer, possibly because the workers came home in contaminated clothes. The exposure went on even after testing went underground. Highly contaminated tunnels had to be cleaned of radioactive debris, irradiated equipment had to be retrieved, and venting after detonations spread radiation everywhere.

Jack Davis worked in the tunnels. His widow remembers him coming home covered with radioactive dust and ashes. She contracted cancer, as had Jack's first wife, who had died of it. Jack became so sick that he had trouble breathing and couldn't walk back out of the tunnels. At his wife's request he was fired from the job. His boss died of cancer a few years later, and Jack died of cancer at the age of forty-nine, but not before his voice box and tongue had been removed in a vain attempt to halt the spread of the disease. Jack's son took work at the NTS, but by age forty-three his legs and back were bothering him and he felt fatigued and dizzy from an ailment that doctors have been unable to identify.[12]

Walter Atkins was at the Baneberry accident, one of the worst of forty or more major leaks of radiation from an underground test. Three hundred feet (90 m) of earth ripped open not far from the mess hall where he was drinking coffee. For twenty-four hours, hot gas and dust shot out of the ground. The radioactive cloud was swept up by a winter storm and came down as snow, contaminating ski slopes hundreds of miles away. Since Atkins had always been told that radiation was not harmful, he didn't take shelter in a tunnel where others hid. He had a hacking cough for the next two years. Later he broke out with skin cancer, a tumor formed in his throat, and then tumors developed in various parts of his body. He had to have a coronary bypass operation to prepare for the removal of a tumor from his lung. Later, the entire lung was removed, and then he died.[13]

WORKERS AND THE MILITARY
IN THE SOUTH PACIFIC

During the testing in Nevada, testing continued in the Pacific as hydrogen bombs were considered too big for testing in the continental United States. The Marshall Islands were seen as a safer test site for these massive explosions and their mountainous mushroom clouds.

The military personnel who conducted the tests and cleaned up afterward on the Bikini Atoll took home a few problems. George Seabron, for example, had helped decontaminate target ships after both the Able and Baker tests. On the trip back to the United States, he recalls, many sailors were very sick. They were told it was sea sickness, which seemed odd for professional sailors. Seabron suffered dizziness, rashes, and headaches, and today still suffers back, bone, and muscle problems and constant pain. Furthermore, he is sterile.[14]

Burney Durkin was one of the sailors who stayed on deck during the tests of Operation Greenhouse in the South Pacific in 1951. When the bombs went off 9 to 13 miles (14 to 21 km) away, he could see the bones of his hands and arms as though he were looking through an X ray. His job was to help scrub down the deck of his ship with sand, stone, and water while most of the crew stayed below deck. He worked in bare feet, with no protective clothing at all. He received beta burns on exposed skin. Fifteen years later he had lymphoma, a type of cancer. His son would die of leukemia in 1983.[15]

Ben Fudge, with the Army on Eniwetok Island in 1955, was ordered to stand on the beach during the Castle series. After one shot, the island was evacuated. He later swam in the lagoon and snorkeled around sunken target ships. A year later he developed a rash that reappeared every year for ten years. Fifteen years later, his teeth and gums were disintegrating. His thyroid completely disintegrated, requiring him to take medication for the rest of his life.[16]

Barry Kail was in the Navy during Operation Hardtack in 1958 when a 4.2-megaton bomb was detonated 250,000 feet (76,000 m) over the Pacific. Within a year, and for the next twenty-five years, he suffered from chronic itching, swelling, and cracking of his feet. He now is plaqued by chronic fatigue, bleeding from the rectum, and problems with his joints, bones, gastrointestinal system, and bronchial tubes.[17]

Again, over the years these "atomic veterans" found it very hard, if not impossible, to claim medical benefits for their problems. Radiation doses were not accurately measured, records were either not kept very carefully or perhaps even deliberately falsified, and the military denied any possible links between the tests and health problems that occurred years later. In the end, the inhabitants of the Marshall Islands received more help and benefits, however inadequate, than the American soldiers, sailors, and airmen who were suffering for their attempts to defend their country.

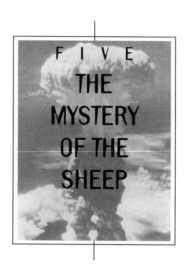

F I V E
THE MYSTERY OF THE SHEEP

By 1953, after two years of testing, downwinders were starting to show concern. Following the first shots in the Upshot-Knothole series, an editorial in the Salt Lake City newspaper *Desert News* called the testing of atomic weapons tragic and insane but admitted that the tests had to go on for the sake of national security. A few days later, an article quoted Dr. Lyle E. Borst, a former director of the AEC's Brookhaven National Laboratory, who found the fallout dangerous. Dr. Borst said that radiation doses were cumulative and that he did not allow his children to play outside after a detonation. "I don't believe in taking chances," he said. "I would no more let my children be exposed to small amounts of radiation unnecessarily than I would let them take small doses of arsenic."[1]

During the tests that followed in April, headlines repeatedly referred to suspicious illnesses. The AEC denied any possible connection between illness and radiation. The level of radiation was far too low to have any effect, it said. Meanwhile, however, uranium prospectors were reporting that their Geiger counters were useless because everything was more radioactive than the ore they were looking for.

By 1954, the AEC recognized that they had a serious public relations problem. In 1955 the Teapot series of tests was coming up. The longest series to date it would include some very large detonations. The AEC solution to the complaints about health problems was to counterattack with a public relations program that sounds today like black humor. The pamphlet, titled "Atomic tests in Nevada," featured a cartoon cowboy sitting on a horse while a mushroom cloud billowed up behind him. The explanations, of grade-school simplicity, clearly stated that the radiation was of no possible danger to any living thing outside of the NTS. "Your best action is not to be worried about fallout," the pamphlet said. "If you are in a fallout area, you will be advised. Please bear in mind that it is extremely unlikely that there will be fallout in any occupied community greater than the past low levels."[2] The pamphlet went on to explain that radiation is a natural part of life (which is true), but by so doing, it implied that levels above normal background levels are natural, normal, and not unhealthy. Cancer was not mentioned as a possible long-term effect of fallout. No measures were suggested for protection from radiation. The only advice offered was to avoid looking directly at the explosion without wearing sunglasses.

The AEC public relations program seems to have been largely successful. Gallup polls taken in the 1950s and 1960s indicated that Americans considered nuclear war a very real possibility. They advocated the development of larger nuclear weapons, supported the atomic tests, and were not worried about radiation.[3] In the 1956 presidential campaign, candidate Adlai Stevenson, who advocated stopping at least the H-bomb tests, lost to General Dwight D. Eisenhower, who was approving every test series the military requested. Nevada and Utah were among the states that supported Eisenhower by a very wide margin.

American voters reelected officials who supported the testing program. Henry "Scoop" Jackson, of Washington State, who was on the Joint Committee on Atomic Energy (JCAE) and strongly supported testing, was reelected to the Senate in every election from 1953 to 1983. Another JCAE member and testing advocate, New Mexico's Clinton Anderson, was reelected to the Senate from 1949 to 1972. Pat McCarran of Nevada, another supporter of the tests despite criticism from his constituents, served in the Senate for twenty years.

The governor of Nevada, Charles Russell, was also for continued testing. The paychecks of thousands of soldiers who came to Nevada and the AEC money spent on local supplies were a boon to the economy of Nevada. In effect, a vast expanse of desert was producing cash. "We had long ago written off that terrain as wasteland," Russell said. "Today it's blooming with atoms."[4] In Las Vegas, gambling businesses, worried that the tests might scare away their customers, tried to turn the tests into a local gag. They offered potent "atomic cocktails," showed a model with an atomic hairdo that resembled a mushroom cloud, and published a picture of a girl in a bikini using a Geiger counter to check the beard of a dusty prospector. Soon people who didn't gamble were coming to Las Vegas just to see the distant flash of an atomic explosion.[5]

When U.S. congressman Douglas Stringfellow of Utah called for the testing to stop, the *Las Vegas Review-Journal* reminded him that atomic testing was the business of Nevada, not Utah.[6] When E. C. Leutzinger, representative of Nevada, called for the testing to stop, that same paper called him a crackpot.[7]

A STRANGE SLAUGHTER OF SHEEP

During the 1953 Upshot-Knothole series, cattle, horses and sheep had been wintering in pastures about 50 miles (80 km) north of the NTS. A few cattle died during the series, and several horses were found to have lesions on their backs. Sheep were especially hard hit, and several thousand died mysteriously. Kern Bullock, a rancher, remembers the incident.

> *We were on the trail home from our Nevada range into our Utah range, and I was out on the saddle horse with this herd of sheep just sitting . . . kind of watching the sheep. They were all grazing, and these airplanes came over . . . and all at once this bomb dropped. . . .*
>
> *I wasn't expecting it. . . . It just was an atomic bomb . . . . And of course, the cloud came up and drifted over us . . . . And, it was a little bit later that day that some of the Army personnel that had four-by-fours and jeeps . . . came through . . . and they said, "Boy, you guys are really in a hot spot."*
>
> *Well, we had to herd the sheep. We had to move as fast as they walked . . . and that's not very fast. . . .*
>
> *We trailed into Cedar City. I guess it was 200 and some odd miles . . . and when we got into our lambing yards . . . we started losing sheep. . . .*
>
> *When they started to lamb, we started losing them, and the lambs were born with little legs, kind of potbellied. As I remember, some of them*

didn't have any wool, kind of a skin instead of wool. . . .

And we just started losing so many lambs that my father . . . just about went crazy. He had never seen anything like it before. Neither had I; neither had anybody else.[8]

In all, 12 percent of the pregnant female sheep in that area died, and a quarter of newborn lambs died within three weeks of Shot Harry.[9] Many lambs were born stunted, half the normal weight, and they died within a week. Many were born with deformities. Sheep had open sores on their snouts. When their wool was shorn, it just separated from their bodies, exposing large scabs.

AEC tests supposedly showed that the amount of radiation received should not have killed the animals.[10] One sheep had liver readings of radiation double normal levels, lung and bone readings four times normal, and thyroid readings one-hundred-fifty times normal, but those levels were somehow considered too low to have killed the animal.[11]

Oddly enough, the AEC inspectors did not examine the gastrointestinal tracts of the dead animals. That part of the animal—and human—body is especially susceptible to radiation, which explains the nausea and diarrhea that people often feel during times of passing fallout. Gastrointestinal examinations might have explained signs of malnutrition in the dead animals.

The AEC convened a meeting of AEC people and federal, state, and scientific consultants to discuss the problem. There was no agreement between the AEC and the others. However, everyone was asked to sign a paper to record their attendance at the meeting. Later, the AEC presented a document with those signatures. The document stated that the signatures attested to the signers' agreement that radiation had not been responsi-ble for the deaths.[12] The signers, however, had never seen that agreement, let alone consented to it.

AEC inspectors determined that the cause of death was malnutrition and the consumption of poisonous plants. The poison, they said, had made the animals' snouts sensitive to light and thus caused burn marks that looked so much like beta burns. An inspector for the state of Utah, a specialist in poisonous plants, said that poisonous plants could not have been the cause of the deaths or the burn marks. Robert Thompsett, a veterinar-ian from the Los Alamos Scientific Laboratory, hesitant-ly said that the injuries looked the same as those of ani-mals injured by the Trinity test. Radiation, he said, was probably the factor that pushed weak, malnourished animals into death.[13]

The American public heard nothing but the AEC side of the story. A *New York Times* article, for example, said that "the commission spared no effort to trace any con-nection between the [atomic] explosions and the mor-tality of the sheep. The commission's Los Alamos, N.M., scientific laboratory . . . set to work exposing test sheep to beta rays to see if the sores matched. They did not. It was established that the sheep could not have gotten more than one-fortieth of the minimum injurious dose [of iodine-131]."[14]

In 1955, several ranchers filed a complaint in feder-al district court against the U.S. government. The AEC presented evidence that the sheep had died of cold, malnutrition, various infectious diseases, and consump-tion of poisonous plants. The ranchers had little to offer as evidence. Veterinarians who had nothing to do with the AEC testified that the cause of death seemed to be radiation. One rancher testified that he had been told the sheep were "hotter than a $2 pistol." But the testi-mony of state and local veterinarians was not as credible as that of government agents who knew more about radiation. The ranchers' reports of comments by AEC people could not be verified. The AEC denials that there were harmful levels of radiation in the area had to be accepted. Judge Sherman Christensen had to decide that the preponderance of evidence was against the sheepmen. The only consolation he gave them was that the government had been negligent, that the AEC had had "the duty to use reasonable care to ascertain whether there were [civilians] within areas to be affected and to at least give them timely warning."[15] The government was found not guilty and not responsible for the losses.[16] Most surprisingly, the deaths of the animals, undeniably suspicious, never led to warnings that similar exposure among humans might be dangerous.

The truth began to come out only twenty-eight years later, in 1979, when the U.S. Congress began to investigate AEC actions during the testing program.

According to the testimony of local ranchers as well as doctors and AEC personnel, the AEC investigation of the deaths was a cover-up. AEC officials were simply seeking data that they could alter or destroy. Dr. Stephen Brower, Iron County agricultural agent, testified:

During the first month or two of the initial investigation, the scientists who were there were, in fact . . . saying and specifying this was radiation damage. . . .

[But] they were taken off the case. In fact, Dr. Thompsett, who said he would give me a copy of the report and provide a copy of his report to the livestock men indicating the readings and the appearance of the animals were similar to an experimental radiation damage done on animals, told me later that this report was picked up, even his own personal copy, and he was

told to rewrite it and eliminate any reference to speculation about radiation damage or effects.[17]

Dr. Brower also testified that Dr. Paul Pearson, then chief of the Biological Branch, Division of Medicine, of the AEC, told him the motivation behind the dishonest investigation.

Dr. Pearson told me . . . that the AEC could under no circumstances afford to have a claim established against them and have that precedent set. And he further indicated that the sheepmen could not expect under any circumstances to be reimbursed for that reason.[18]

Dr. Harold Knapp, a scientist who worked for the AEC Fallout Studies Branch and who conducted health surveys of the effects of radiation on people, inspected the sheep. He noted facts quite different from those of the AEC inspectors.

The simplest explanation of the primary cause of death in the lambing ewes is irradiation of the ewe's gastrointestinal (GI) tract by beta particles from all the fission products that were ingested by the sheep along with open range forage. . . . The internal radiation doses to the GI tract of adult sheep are calculated to be in the thousands of rads, even though the external gamma dose was within the 3.9 rad limit set per test series established with the AEC acceptable for persons living in areas adjacent to the test site.

The death of the newborn lambs may be attributed to serious damage to their thyroids from doses in the range of 20,000 to 40,000 rads from isotopes of radioiodine present in the fallout from the 24 March 1953 test (Nancy), and ingested by the pregnant ewes 40–60 days prior to birth.[19]

Dr. Knapp also testified that the government had known beforehand that evidence of low external doses could indicate very high internal doses. By eating contaminated food and water, the animals concentrated the fallout inside their bodies. Much of the fallout would remain there, continuously radiating long after the radioactive cloud had passed. The government also knew that iodine-131 eaten by pregnant ewes could be deadly to fetuses. Nonetheless, the AEC carefully avoided any questions or investigations that would bring this information to light.

Although he had no witnesses to back him up, a rancher testified that a deputy test site manager had said to him, "Joe, the easiest thing we could do would be to pay for these sheep, but if we paid for them, every woman that got pregnant and every woman that didn't would sue us."[20]

The issue of precedent was all-important to the AEC. If it was held responsible for the deaths of sheep, it could all the more easily be held responsible for the deaths of people. Whether the AEC feared this as a real possibility is not known, but certainly every doctor and scientist in the world knew that radiation could be dangerous and that a lot of it was exploding into the skies of Nevada.

SIX
THE DISASTROUS EFFECTS ON HEALTH

In the late 1950s, people in Utah and Nevada became alarmed by the increased incidence of cancer and leukemia. Before the testing, leukemia had been virtually unknown in those states. In a few cases, local doctors misdiagnosed it because they had never seen it before.[1] Soon, however, leukemia became commonplace. In 1960, four teenagers died in Parowan, Utah, a village with a population of a few hundred. Normally, only a population of 200,000 would experience so many fatal cases of leukemia.[2] When Blaine Johnson's daughter came down with leukemia in Cedar City, Utah, he asked a doctor if it wasn't unusual to have seven cases within a hundred yards of his house.[3] Washington, Utah, with a population of only 450, suffered six leukemia deaths by the 1960s. Gloria Gregerson, of Bunkerville, Nevada, noted that of the fifty families she knew in her town, only four did not have someone dead or dying of cancer. One family had seven cancers and twelve miscarriages. When Jay Truman went to his high school reunion, he discovered that he was the only one among nine friends who had survived to the age of twenty-eight.[4] When a regular flood of cancer victims started coming in, Elmer Pickett, a mortician, had to look for books on how to properly embalm them. He had never seen a case of cancer in his mortuary. Before long, cancer struck nine people in his own family, the first cases in his family in several generations.[5]

In 1979, at a congressional hearing, Martha Laird spoke for many downwinders when she said, "I feel that we were more or less used as guinea pigs. The forgotten guinea pigs, because guinea pigs they will come to the cage and check, which they never have. To this day, they have never checked anyone in my family or anyone I know of from the fallout of these bombs."[6]

Among the probable victims of fallout were many of the 220-member crew of a John Wayne movie, *The Conqueror*. The filming took place in 1955 in a canyon 12 miles (19 km) west of St. George. The crew used huge fans to simulate wind, a deadly special effect. The wind blew up clouds of radioactive dust, which was inhaled by the crew and stuck to the makeup on the faces of the actors. Even worse, when some of the scenes had to be reshot, the studio had 60 tons of dirt delivered to a set in Hollywood. Among the actors, Susan Hayward, Agnes Moorehead, Dick Powell, and John Wayne, eventually all died of cancer. By 1983, ninety-one of the crew had developed cancer.[7]

The concerns of the local citizens of Utah and Nevada were eventually supported by several well-informed and widely recognized scientists, among them five future Nobel laureates. Dr. Joshua Lederberg warned that not enough was known about the effects of low-level radiation.[8] Dr. Linus Pauling held that the effects of radiation were far worse and more widespread than the AEC acknowledged. In 1957 he said that 10,000 people had contracted leukemia because of the testing.[9] In 1958 he said that the tests so far would "ultimately produce about 1 million seriously defective children and about 1 million embryonic and neonatal deaths, and will cause many millions of people to suffer from hereditary diseases.[10] Dr. Hermann Muller feared worldwide genetic damage due to radiation from tests. The AEC, however, never publicly admitted the possibility that any of these scientists might be right.[11] A third Nobel scientist, Dr. Andrei Sakharov, who had invented the Soviet hydrogen bomb, said that, "because of the fallout of the radioactive products of nuclear explosions in the atmosphere, every megaton claims thousands of lives." By his reasoning, if over 585 megatons had been exploded in the atmosphere by 1958, millions may have died throughout the world.[12] At that time, only slightly more than half of atmospheric tests had been conducted. Dr. Albert Schweitzer, while not a nuclear scientist, also warned that the tests were killing people and should be terminated.[13]

From the 1950s to the 1990s, both Dr. John Gofman and Dr. Ernest Sternglass have been extremely concerned about the effects of radiation. They also claim that the federal government and people supported by government funding have been either lying about what is known, carefully investigating only areas where no harm will show up, or preventing the further study of what could be learned.[14]

Dr. Gofman codiscovered uranium-235 and isolated the world's first milligram of plutonium. He has written definitive works on the effects of radiation, especially low-dose radiation. In contradiction to many studies, he claims that radiation can cause all forms of cancer and that the danger of fatal radiation-related cancers is about three times higher than the U.S. government admits.[15] He says there is a direct correlation between the level of prenatal exposure to radiation and mental capacity after birth. He believes severe mental retardation occurs in almost half of fetuses exposed to 100 rad between the eighth and fifteenth week of pregnancy.

Dr. Gofman, who was a valued director of a biomedical division at the government-run Livermore laboratories, claims that with almost all nuclear research funded by the government, scientists are not truly independent and research projects that might question the safety of radiation are not funded. In 1969, in a paper titled "Low-Dose Radiation, Cancer and Chromosomes," he asserted that the risk of radiation-induced cancer is twenty times higher than estimated and that if everyone in the United States received the maximum allowable dose of radiation, 16,000 to 32,000 people would die. According to Gofman, the chairman of the Joint Committee on Atomic Energy said to him, "Listen, there have been others who have tried to cross the AEC before you. We got them and we'll get you."[16]

The AEC cut off Gofman's funding at Livermore, and in several other incidents the AEC apparently prevented his research. Dr. Gofman asserts that the effects of the testing are far worse than the government admits, that radiation exposure doses were far higher than acknowledged, and that the effects per rad of exposure are worse than generally believed.[17]

Dr. Ernest Sternglass has also been a consistent, long-term critic of nuclear testing and government attempts to hide the results of those tests. A professor of radiation physics at the University of Pittsburgh Medical School, Sternglass first rocked the boat in 1969 with articles published in The Bulletin of the Atomic Scientists and Esquire magazine, both on the same topic. They reported that in the first half of the century infant mortality had been declining throughout the United States. As soon as the nuclear test program started in Nevada, however, that decline in New York State leveled off. As soon as the testing stopped, the death rate there resumed its decline. Meanwhile, in states upwind of the NTS, such as California, the decline had continued unabated.[18] In the *Esquire* article he stated, "The scientific evidence indicates that *already* at least one of three children who died before their first birthdays in America in the 1960s, may have died as a result of peacetime nuclear testing."[19]

HEALTH STUDIES

Despite these warnings from respected scientists, no accurate, comprehensive surveys of radiation exposures or effects were conducted by any government agency, and what data existed was virtually useless. Fallout maps were inaccurate. Cloud tracking had been incomplete. Monitoring equipment was off by as much as 30 percent. Readings were taken not far from roads, and monitoring covered too few places to record the many "hot spots" and "cold spots" that could be, respectively, twice or half the reading taken at a spot a few yards away.[20]

Dr. Harold Knapp, a former AEC specialist in fallout, said there was "indirect, tenuous but troublesome evidence that such hot spots may in fact have existed and resulted in actual doses of up to 50 rad to persons as far away as 100 miles (160 km) from the test site. The crude dosimeters [that] provide such evidence are people and sheep."[21] By that he meant the immediate effects on people and sheep, "the loss of hair, the skin burns, the nausea," served to indicate the presence of high levels of radiation. The AEC permissible maximum of 3 rad would not cause such effects. Fifty rad would be closer to the truth.

A great deal of the inaccuracy could be attributed to a total lack of estimates of internal doses, that is, radioactive particles inhaled or swallowed, the most dangerous form of radiation. Since some of the particles are chemically similar to the nutrients that the body stores, the atoms can become part of the body. Consider, for example, the radioactive substances strontium-90 and iodine-131. Strontium-90, similar to the nutrient calcium, readily attaches itself to bone. Iodine-131 accumulates in the thyroid, just like common iodine, which is necessary for good health. Once part of the body, such particles emit radiation point-blank. The big, heavy alpha particles, which cannot penetrate skin, are especially dangerous as they radiate adjacent tissue.

The problem here is that to study the causes of cancer, epidemiologists need to know who was exposed to what. Without that information, it is very difficult to link a cause and an effect.

The first significant medical study that suggested a connection between radioactive fallout from nuclear tests and human disease, "Leukemia Mortality Studies in Southwestern Utah," was conducted by Dr. Edward Weiss, a biostatistician with the Public Health Service. He counted the deaths from leukemia in two rural Utah counties between 1950 and 1960 and compared the number with the total leukemia deaths in Brooklyn, New York. Dr. Weiss found that the rate for all types of leukemia in one of the Utah counties, Washington County, was 1.46 times higher than in Brooklyn in the same period. The leukemia death rate for people under the age of nineteen was 3.29 times higher. The report was not thorough or perfectly done, however, and the AEC criticized it sharply. Although the study did not explicitly link leukemia with fallout, the AEC feared that people, especially people in the federal government, would leap to that conclusion. According to a congressional report issued in 1980, the AEC was worried that the conclusions would have detrimental effects upon the government's nuclear weapons program.[22] Dr.

Weiss's superiors at the Public Health Service decided not to let him publish it, or to pursue further studies in that area. The original report was not made public until a reporter requested it under the Freedom of Information Act years later.[23]

Dr. Harold Knapp had received information that infants in St. Louis, 1,800 miles (2,900 km) from the NTS, were found to have shockingly high levels of radioactive iodine-131 in their thyroids. The only existing exposure data indicated that they might have received only a few hundredths of 1 rad of external radiation from the passing of a cloud from Nevada. Their thyroids, however, proved to be exposed to 2 rad of internal radiation. Dr. Knapp suspected that if infants in St. Louis had received so much radioactive iodine-131, people closer to the test site must have received a tremendous amount.

Dr. Knapp's study specifically looked at milk as the means of transmitting the iodine-131 to people. The iodine had landed on grass, and cows had eaten the grass. The iodine became concentrated in the cows' milk. When people drank the milk, their thyroids concentrated it even more. Unfortunately, until 1957, to monitor iodine-131 in milk, the AEC had bought just 1 quart (about 1 l) off a grocery shelf, then lost it in the laboratory. Since that particular isotope has a half-life of only eight days, iodine-131 disintegrates beyond detection within three months.[24]

Dr. Knapp concluded that the thyroids of children drinking a quart of milk a day could have received doses as high as 440 rad, an amount thousands of times higher than anything the AEC had ever reported.[25]

The AEC immediately called Dr. Knapp's report into question. The AEC called together several top scientists from AEC laboratories, who said that Dr. Knapp should publish his evidence and let the scientific community decide if he was right or wrong. Reluctantly, the AEC allowed the report to be published. Unfortunately, however, the published version failed to include a key section that described how Shot Harry alone had exposed some children's thyroids to 120 to 440 rad.[26]

Did the AEC know that iodine-131 was contaminating food, entering the food chain, and possibly harming human health as an internal source of radiation exposure? A Congressional hearing in 1979 revealed two sides to the story. Richard Stanley, deputy director of the U.S. Environmental Monitoring and Support Laboratory, testified that the AEC had not known of the dangers of iodine-131 and internal doses during the years of atmospheric testing, when, he said, "analytical equipment and techniques weren't adequately developed for the identification and measurement of [iodine-131]. Consequently, [iodine-131] wasn't recognized as a potential problem, and no protective actions were taken to minimize thyroid doses resulting from the ingestion of milk contaminated with radioiodine. . . ."[27]

At the same hearings, however, Dr. Joseph Lyons of the University of Utah said that the AEC knew of the potential hazards of radiation taken in with food. "In 1953, Mr. Weiss [a researcher with the Public Health Service] cited monitor's reports in the St. George area [that] were very concerned about the milk, went so far as to sample the milk, actually took it back to Las Vegas; and then given the lack of knowledge, did attempt an analysis on the nuclide levels of iodine. So there was some awareness of this. . . . My impression was that there must have been some awareness of a risk factor and yet nothing ever seems to be pursued to the end where you can get the precise information . . . we need for our scientific studies."[28]

Dr. Knapp, who had studied fallout for the AEC, testified that in 1963, as an intense series of tests was beginning, he realized how inaccurate AEC estimates of iodine-131 doses had been. "For eleven years we had missed by a factor of 100 to 1,000, perhaps, the doses to the thyroid of infants and young children that drank milk from cows that were grazing downwind in the fall-out areas around the Nevada Test Site." He also said that the AEC Division of Operational Safety had dragged its feet to prevent his report from being published. When he suggested changing the guidelines for protecting the public from radiation, the commission refused. An AEC memorandum stated, "To change the guides would require a re-education program that could raise questions in the public mind as to the validity of the past guides. . . . Therefore we recommend the continuation of the present criteria."[29]

The first study to link leukemia with radiation, "Childhood Leukemia Associated with Fallout from the Nuclear Testing," was concluded by Dr. Joseph Lyons in 1979. He compared the number of deaths in high-fall-out counties and low-fallout counties before, during, and after the testing period. He found that the death rate in the counties receiving the highest exposure was 2.44 times higher than expected. When the geographic areas were further subdivided, those counties closest to the NTS had death rates 3.4 times higher than the counties farthest away.[30]

Dr. Charles E. Land of the National Cancer Institute was critical of Dr. Lyons' study. He said the study found no correlation between bone marrow dose and leukemia and that the high-exposure population showed a decrease in other kinds of childhood cancer. He also said that the results of the study depended on the relatively low leukemia rate before the testing period. Since the rate was low then, it only appeared to be higher during the tests. The rate was low, he said, because the one doctor who had been serving 125,000 people in seventeen counties simply had not been able to diagnose all the cases.[31] That point of criticism, however, did not explain why the rate decreased to its earlier rate after the testing stopped.

In 1980 Dr. Glyn Caldwell, of the Centers for Disease Control, looked for leukemia among veterans who had participated in maneuvers in the vicinity of Shot Smokey in 1957. Dr. Caldwell's study was in response to the case of Paul Cooper, one of the soldiers who had advanced to ground zero immediately after the explosion. Twenty years later, Cooper contracted leukemia. He claimed that the disease was caused by his exposure to radiation, but the Veterans Administration saw no such connection.

Dr. Caldwell contacted most of the 3,224 participants who had witnessed the shot. It turned out that 9 of them had died of leukemia while statistically only 3.5 could have been expected to die. The oddest finding, however, was that according to the records, the men had received very low doses of radiation—0.5 to 1.0 rad—too little to have caused leukemia. Estimating the likelihood that 70 rad would be needed to produce the effects found, Dr. Caldwell concluded that either the doses were actually much higher than recorded or that doses much lower than expected could cause leukemia. In the study Dr. Caldwell stated that he had found no other possible source of the leukemia.[32]

The federally sponsored Brookhaven National laboratory criticized Dr. Caldwell's study, saying that the number of people studied was not large enough to justify a statistical conclusion. It also refused to accept the possibility that exposures had exceeded 1 rad, because that was the highest reading on the film badges the soldiers had worn.[33]

Three years later, Dr. Caldwell did a follow-up study.

This time he found that general cancer rates were actually a bit *lower* than expected. There were 112 cases of cancer where 117 were expected. Leukemia, however, was substantially more common than expected: 10 cases observed where 4 were expected, with 8 deaths where only 3.1 were expected. Dr. Caldwell acknowledged that the results could not be generalized to apply to people outside the study. [34]

Two federal employees, Harold Beck and Philip Krey, tried to reconstruct probable exposures by testing soil samples for cesium-137 at one-hundred-fifty sites across the state of Utah. To everyone's surprise, they found that people in northern Utah, which is further from the NTS, had received an average exposure 50 percent higher than people in southern Utah. The only exception was in Washington County, which is the county closest to the NTS. The average dose in the high-fallout regions was 0.3 rad, far too little to cause leukemia. Their conclusion was that the Lyons study was invalid.[35]

Subsequently, Dr. Carl J. Johnson found a clear link between exposure to radiation and all kinds of cancer. In 1981, he compared the health of people who in 1951 had been living in the most highly exposed areas in southern Utah and people who lived throughout Utah in that year. A total of 4,125 people were involved, all Mormons, the vast majority of whom did not smoke or drink. The study assessed not only their probable exposure but also their lifestyles.

The conclusions were clear-cut. The average cancer rate in Utah would have predicted 179 cases in southern Utah, but 288 were observed. Leukemia in the more highly exposed group occurred sooner than expected and persisted longer. Cancer of the thyroid gland was more common among the highly exposed. The study also predicted increasing cancer rates throughout Utah because leukemia rates were already higher than for the rest of the country. Generally, cancer rates rise after leukemia rates rise.

Most startling was the increase in the rates of *all* kinds of cancer. The incidence of leukemia had been 5.3 times above the normal rate from 1958 to 1966, then 3.5 times above normal from 1972 to 1980. In that latter period, incidence of lymphoma was 1.9 times above normal rates, thyroid cancer was 8.2 times, breast cancer 1.9 times, colon cancer 1.7 times above normal, stomach cancer 1.8 times, melanoma 3.5 times, brain cancer was 1.7 times, and the incidence of cancer of the bones and joints was a horrifying 12.5 times above normal rates.[36]

This study, too, came under criticism. Testifying before the Senate in 1990, Dr. Lyons said that the Johnson study was not backed up by death certificates and that there was evidence that "the individuals included in the study had been selected to substantially overstate the number of cancers that might have occurred."[37]

During that same Senate hearing, Dr. Lyons was asked "the extent to which [his] research in this area [was] delayed and complicated by government failure to monitor the fallout exposure levels experienced by our citizens in Utah." Dr. Lyons responded, "We started out with virtually no dose estimates, and it has taken several years for the government to actually find data necessary to make dose estimates."[38] Although it was not stated, the implication was that by not keeping records on exposure and then delaying the providing of what records existed, the AEC was protecting itself from blame. No one would be able to link their cancer to radiation, at least not easily.

In their book *Deadly Deceit,* authors Jay M. Gould and Benjamin A. Goldman reviewed national statistics from the Public Health Service and found some disturbing trends. When they looked at infant mortality—the rate at which the newborn die—they found that in general, since the nineteenth century, the mortality rate has been declining. Each year, fewer babies have died in their first year. This trend has no doubt been due to improvements in living conditions and health care.[39]

The authors also looked at infant mortality from 1930 to 1985. The average number of infant deaths per 100,000 people was over 60 in 1930 and just under 15 in 1985. The decline was generally steady *except* during the 1950s and early 1960s, when the number declined so slowly it almost leveled off. As soon as the United States and Soviet Union stopped atmospheric testing, the decline resumed its faster rate. The general decline and temporary leveling-off applied to deaths of people of all ages. Mortality declined about 2 percent per year, but during the years of atmospheric testing, mortality declined by an average of only 0.8 percent per year. The higher rate resumed when the testing stopped. According to a 1968 report from the Harvard School of Public Health, there was no reason to expect infant mortality to stop declining at that point in history, and in fact an improvement could have been expected.[40] An article in the *American Journal of Public Health* noted that low birth weights, a chief cause of neonatal death, increased by 10 percent among white babies and 50 percent among nonwhite babies from 1950 to 1963. The percentage has been slowly declining since then.[41]

THE PLUTONIUM EXPERIMENTS

Bombs were not the only source of government-issued radiation. In the mid-1940s, in a highly secret program, for purely experimental purposes, the U.S. government injected eighteen human subjects with plutonium. The main objective was to see how fast the body would cleanse itself of that extremely dangerous substance.

The youngest was a boy not yet five years old. Another child was of an age not known today, and one young lady was eighteen. Several of the subjects were in their sixties. All of the subjects were thought to be terminally ill. Some had cancer. One was suffering from several fatal symptoms of alcoholism. One was a hemophiliac, one suffered from Cushing's syndrome, one suffered from Hodgkin's disease, and one had Addison's disease. None were expected to live long enough for the plutonium to cause yet another disease. Surprisingly enough, some of them lived for decades and died at a respectably old age.

Apparently only one of the subjects was informed of the experiment, and even he probably had no idea of how dangerous it was. Some of the others may have received an oral explanation and given oral permission. For such a serious and life-threatening experiment, that consent, if it was actually given, would not be considered legal today.

Little is known of the people involved in these human experiments. *The Albuquerque Tribune,* after exhausting and persistent investigation, managed to determine the identities of five of the eighteen people.[42] The *Tribune's* investigative reporter, Eileen Welsome, who won a Pulitzer Prize for her work, was able to find a little information about each person. The government had given each had a code name, such as CAL-1, CAL-2, CAL-3, CHI-1, HP-2, and in some cases the true identity is still unknown. Welsome determined the date and quantity of each injection, the cause and date of death, and what, if any, posthumous examinations were performed. The posthumous examinations were to determine how much plutonium remained in the body and in what organs and tissues it had remained.

It cannot be denied that government experiments had some beneficial effects. They result in the largest source of data on the effects of plutonium on human health. Now, when radiological workers are contaminated with plutonium, doctors can determine their dose by examining urine and fecal material. They can also be aware how the plutonium will circulate in the blood and where it is likely to settle.

But does the end justify the means? Was the experiment worth the risk to the patients and the agony that some of them may have suffered? Some doctors and radiologists have criticized the experiment not only on moral grounds but on scientific grounds as well. The number of people in the experiment was too small to allow valid conclusions. Some of the patients already suffered from kidney and liver dysfunctions, which would alter their bodies' ability to get rid of a contaminant at a normal rate. Also, it is known that plutonium is most dangerous when inhaled. That, and swallowing, would be the most common ways that people receive an internal dose of plutonium. It would never be accidentally injected by hypodermic needle.

More terrifying than the use of unknowing humans as laboratory animals has been the continuing effort to hide information about the experiment. The secrecy began with a memo issued in 1947 that said, "It is desired that no document be released [that] refers to experiments with humans and might have an adverse effect on public opinion or result in legal suits. Documents covering such work in this field should be classified 'secret.'"[43]

The Department of Energy (DOE), which took over the responsibilities of the AEC in 1977, is still keeping much information secret. The experiments were report-ed in 1976, but no information was released by the AEC or the DOE until *The Albuquerque Tribune* began in-vestigating.

The DOE did not make the discovery easy. The *Tri-bune* and its attorneys have made repeated requests for information that should be readily available under the Freedom of Information Act. Over the course of four years, the DOE delayed and sent irrelevant documents, documents already publicly available, and multiple copies of documents already sent. The DOE inspector general said that he could find no documents to fit the *Tribune's* request. When the *Tribune* appealed, the DOE Office of Hearings and Appeals replied that the inspec-tor general's search had been adequate. When a con-gressional representative asked the DOE to be more helpful, it provided documents that were widely avail-able and provided nothing about follow-up examina-tions in the 1970s of surviving patients or the remains of the deceased. Finally, after four years of efforts, the DOE sent five previously unseen documents, one of which contained the name of one patient.

In 1993, the *Tribune* was still demanding that the names be released. Hazel O'Leary, secretary of the DOE, said that the information would be released as soon as department attorneys advised her on the legali-ty of releasing the information. The department claims that it cannot find much of the information. Some of that information includes 250 documents produced during an inquiry into the matter in the 1970s. It has not been determined whether the documents have been lost, destroyed, or hidden.

Many more people have been injured by govern-ment experiments. In October 1995, a President's Advi-sory Committee on Human Radiation Experiments handed President Clinton a 900-page report on 4,000 experiments conducted on 16,000 people.[44] It found misrepresentation of facts and efforts to cover up the truth about the plutonium experiments. It also reported tests on human subjects by the Public Health Administration, the National Aeronautics and Space Administration, the Department of Veterans Affairs, the Central Intelligence Agency, and the Department of Defense. One experiment released large amounts of radioactive materials near populated areas. Another exposed individuals to strong X-ray doses. Some experiments tested the reaction of the human eye to an atomic flash of light. The testicles of 133 prisoners in Oregon were irradiated. At Vanderbilt University, 820 pregnant women were given small doses of radioactive iron. Hundreds of children in a school for the mentally retarded were injected with iodine-131. In 1956 and 1957, the U.S. Air Force injected radioactive iodine into 120 people, most of them Eskimos and American Indians. The report on all these experiments recommended that only nine cases clearly called for compensation to the victims.[45] President Clinton issued a general apology to all of the people who were subjected to the experiments, saying, "We will no longer hide the truth from our citizens."[46]

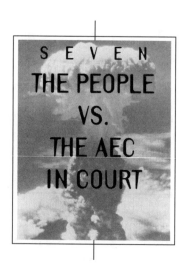

THE PEOPLE
VS.
THE AEC
IN COURT

Long after nuclear weapons stopped exploding over America, the battle continued in federal courts and Congress. Sheep ranchers wanted compensation for the deaths of over 17,000 sheep. Veterans wanted compensation for alleged radiation-related injuries. Local citizens wanted compensation for the cases of cancer and leukemia allegedly caused by the fallout on their towns, homes, food, and bodies.

Despite the commonly acknowledged link between radiation and cancer and the many instances of people and animals affected by radiation, little progress has been made on the legal front. The reasons are many and very complex.

Perhaps the main obstacle has been a doctrine known as sovereign immunity. This doctrine dates back to principles established under the rule of kings in England, when it was held that "the king can do no wrong,"—that is, whatever he did was, by definition, right and good. Over the years, this policy evolved into the right of the American government to be immune from certain liabilities. The government could not be sued unless it gave the injured person permission to do so.

To ease the unfair power of this doctrine, in 1946 the Federal Tort Claims Act (FTCA) was passed. It allows people to sue the government for negligence in certain cases. The FTCA includes a key exception, however, called discretionary function. This exception has never been clearly defined by Congress or the courts. Essentially, it frees the government from suits brought on by the actions of government employees who are following government policy in a reasonably careful way. In such cases, the doctrine of sovereign immunity applies, and the government cannot be held responsible.

The FCTA established other requirements that would make it especially hard for atomic veterans and down-winders to sue the AEC. To succeed, a suit would have to prove that:

1. The government had a legal obligation to act a certain way.
2. Government agents did not act according to their duty.
3. Government agents had a legal obligation to act for the plaintiff's benefit but failed to do so.
4. The plaintiff was actually injured.
5. The action of the government caused the injury.

It would be very hard for people injured by radiation to prove all of these points. Government secrecy would make it difficult to know how its agents had acted. The difficulty of linking radiation to specific cases of cancer would make it hard to prove that plaintiffs had been injured by radiation and that government actions had caused the injury.

The Freedom of Information Act (FOIA), passed in 1966, made many documents of the federal government available to the public. It was modified in 1974 to make it easier for the public to demand and receive documents. From the AEC came reports, memos, warnings, exposure readings, and other data that revealed a dangerous duplicity.

The AEC controlled all nuclear activities until 1974, when it was abolished and its functions split between the Nuclear Regulatory Commission (NRC) and the Energy Research and Development Commission (ERDC). The NRC oversaw regulation and licensing of nuclear power plants. The ERDC handled development of all kinds of energy. The functions of the ERDC were given to the U.S. Department of Energy (DOE) when it was created in 1977. Any controversy over testing done under the AEC is now the domain of the DOE.

In 1978, Congressman Tim Lee Carter, a former doctor from Kentucky who had lost a son to leukemia, organized hearings of the House Subcommittee on Public Health and the Environment. For the first time, AEC officials admitted that mistakes had been made. The public, having recently witnessed the duplicity behind the war in Vietnam and the Nixon administration's Watergate case, was ready to hear about lies and negligence in the AEC.[1]

Following these hearings, President Jimmy Carter formed a task force to look into the relationship between radiation and health. It failed to identify radiation as a cause of cancer or leukemia, but it did suggest further studies. A subsequent task force looked into the possibility of compensating radiation victims who lived downwind from the NTS. No legislation or compensation resulted from either of these investigations.

In 1979, the House Subcommittee on Oversight and

Investigation of the Committee on Interstate and Foreign Commerce held hearings that led to a report called "The Forgotten Guinea Pigs."[2] The hearings heard testimony from: citizens who lived downwind from the test site; doctors who had conducted studies of health effects; AEC officials who either denied or confirmed various reports of negligence; lies, and cover-ups, ranchers whose sheep had died, and others.

On the deaths of the sheep, testimony produced evidence that the AEC witnesses had lied in court and had illegally altered or withheld information that would have helped the sheepmen's case. Internal doses had been ignored or information about them withheld for the sole purpose of preventing any legal connection between radiation and the deaths of sheep. There were indications that the AEC had decided beforehand that, regardless of any facts, the investigation would have to prove that radiation was not at fault because the precedent would lead to more lawsuits, some inevitably resulting from human deaths.[3]

That congressional report concluded that:

1. The government, having sufficient reason to know of the hazards associated with radiation exposure, inexcusably failed to give adequate warning to the sheepmen regarding the danger posed by the nuclear radiation emitted during the 1953 Upshot-Knothole nuclear test series;

2. The government knowingly disregarded and suppressed evidence correlating the deaths of the sheep to exposure to radioactive fallout emitted during [that] series;

3. Exposure to radioactive fallout emitted during [that] series was, more likely than not, the cause of the 1953 sheep deaths in Utah and Nevada;

4. The government wrongly denied compensation to the sheep ranchers for losses incurred as a result of the government's operation of the nuclear testing program.[4]

In 1982, aware of distinct and crucial differences between what had been heard in his court and what was later heard before Congress, Judge Sherman Christensen held hearings on reconsidering the issue of the sheep deaths (see Chapter Five). Following those hearings he concluded that his court had been the victim of "conduct by the government that amounted to a species of fraud upon [the] court," that "improper means" had been used, that "the processes of the court were manipulated to the improper and unacceptable advantage of the defendant," that "evidence was wrongfully withheld," that witnesses were improperly pressured, and that interrogatories (questions that a court requires to be answered) were answered deceptively.[5]

With all that behind his reasoning, Judge Christensen retracted his 1956 decision, ordered the government to pay all costs for that earlier trial, and recommended that the case be heard by an appeals court. In 1983, however, the U.S. Court of Appeals reversed Judge Christensen's decision. Despite the information coming out of the congressional hearings a few years earlier, the appeals court concluded that the hearings had not produced evidence of fraud, that no veterinarians had been pressured to deny the truth, and that no information had been hidden or falsified. The appeal was again rejected by the full appeals court in 1985. The ranchers went to the Supreme Court, which refused to hear the case.

"The Forgotten Guinea Pigs" also probed the effects of radiation on humans. The report's conclusions were every bit as serious as those regarding sheep.

1. The government, though knowing of the hazards of radiation, failed to give adequate warning to residents downwind from the NTS.

2. The radiation monitoring system was deficient in giving estimates accurate enough to protect residents.

3. The government falsely interpreted and reported radiation exposure rates in order to give residents inaccurate estimates of danger.

4. The government knowingly disregarded evidence of the inadequacy of measurements of radiation and radiation safety standards.

5. The fallout from NTS detonations was, more likely than not, responsible for serious health problems among residents downwind from the site.

Just as Congress was holding those hearings, the first big trial on alleged human injury by radiation began to take shape. It started in 1979 with an exhaustive assessment of 1,200 cases of cancer and leukemia. The plaintiffs' attorneys, Stewart Udall and Dale Haralson, sifted through them to find twenty-four that seemed clearly caused by radiation. The individuals had been present when fallout swept across their communities, and their cancers were of the type known to be caused by radiation. Because her name came first alphabetically, Irene Allen's name was used to name the case *Allen et al.* v. *United States.* The *et al.* referred to the other twenty-three plaintiffs.

The plaintiffs charged that the government and its agents had acted negligently in the testing of nuclear weapons at the Nevada Test Site. They alleged that the tests were conducted unsafely, allowing radiation to spread to populated areas. People in those areas were not informed of the danger of radiation or its presence in their communities and their food. They made their charges under the FTCA, charging that they were suing because the government and its agents had not acted in compliance with their duty. The negligence was not policy. The doctrine of sovereign immunity, they said, did not apply.

The government felt that sovereign immunity most certainly did apply and that the "discretionary function" exception to the FTCA freed the government from responsibility for its actions. Besides that, the federal government maintained that no negligence had occurred and that there was no "direct legal causality" between the tests and the illnesses, that is, no scientific proof that a given test had caused a given case of cancer. On those grounds, the government asked that the case be dismissed without trial.

When Judge Bruce Jenkins rejected the request for dismissal, the plaintiffs suggested an out-of-court settlement. The government attorneys steadfastly refused. They could not allow any admission of guilt because there were hundreds or thousands of other cases that might some day come to trial. For the sake of the U.S. Treasury, they wanted a firm court decision of innocence that would discourage any additional trials.[6]

After three years of digging up evidence, the trial began in 1982. The plaintiffs pleaded, and the judge agreed, that, to prove causation, a specific atomic explosion did not have to be scientifically linked to a specific case of cancer. A strong probability linking the tests and the illness would suffice.

The testimony of Dr. Joseph Lyons, who, as we saw in Chapter Six, had conducted a survey that found higher cancer and leukemia rates in downwind communities, did much to bolster the plaintiffs' arguments. He said that childhood leukemia had risen 40 percent in

Utah, and that death by leukemia in the downwind communities was 2.4 percent higher than in the rest of Utah. In the towns closest to the test site, the rate was 3.4 times higher. He therefore saw a 71 percent chance that a given case of leukemia was caused by radiation coming from the test site.[7]

Among the key witnesses was Frank Butrico, the radiation monitor who had been in St. George when the fallout from Shot Harry blew by. His testimony hinted at the deviousness of AEC practices. He said that the AEC had altered reports that had indicated excessive levels of radiation and that he had never been informed what levels were really considered safe or advised what to do in an emergency like the one he faced in St. George. A report issued in 1953 under his name contained inaccurate information and had not in fact been prepared by him. The report said he had been where he hadn't been and that children were safely inside their school when the radiation passed while in fact they had been outside for recess. It said he had taken readings of 3.9 roentgens, precisely the maximum allowed by the AEC, while in fact the readings had been 11.5 roentgens.[8]

Twice during the trial the government asked that the case be dismissed without further argument. Both times the reasons given were that the discretionary function exception excluded the government from responsibility, that the plaintiffs were not successfully linking supposed cause and effect, and that the statute of limitations had already passed (the plaintiffs were suing too long after the bombs were tested).

Judge Jenkins, however, let the trial continue. He wanted all the details and arguments brought forth and put on record for two reasons: the case would surely be appealed, and it would be a landmark decision on the issue of discretionary function.

The four-month trial produced 6,852 pages of transcribed testimony and 54,000 pages of documentation.

It took Judge Jenkins seventeen months to write his 489-page opinion. He rejected the statute of limitations argument because the plaintiffs had not known of their cancer until years after the bomb tests. He accepted the probable link between radiation and ten of the cases of cancer.

Judge Jenkins rejected the discretionary function exception. To illustrate, he used an imaginary situation with the following illustration:

> *Suppose a high-level decision maker says, "International pressures make open-air testing highly necessary. Time is of the essence. We cannot tell our people. We just need to do it and do it as fast as we can. We know as a result of such testing some people are going to get hurt. We can't even warn them what to do to minimize or prevent the hurt. In order to preserve our way of life some people unknown to them or unknown to us are going to give their all for the good of all."*[9]

If that imaginary situation had been real, the discretionary function exception would have applied because what actually came to happen would have been established at the policy level. Agents could be said to have done as they were told. That would free them from charges of negligence. The federal policy, however, was quite the opposite of Jenkins's hypothetical scenario. By policy, the tests were supposed to be safe. The government claimed precautions would be taken. But that did not happen. In contrast to the imaginary government's actions, those of the AEC were desperate and careless.

So in all, ten people were awarded compensation. The other thirteen had not adequately established a connection between the tests and their illnesses. In some cases their cancers were of a type supposedly not caused by radiation. In other cases the victims were seen as not exposed to enough radiation to have caused cancer. One death from skin cancer was attributed to too much sun. A man's death from stomach cancer was not attributable to radiation because a study of the downwind area found no increase in stomach cancer among males. Two deaths from lung cancer were not attributed to radiation because surveys in Hiroshima and Nagasaki had found no increase in lung cancer there. A man who died of cancer of the pancreas was assumed to have contracted it from smoking two packs of cigarettes a day.

The monetary awards were quite low by modern standards, however. Even though the court found that the tests had killed ten people, the spouses of those who died of leukemia were awarded $240,000. A son or daughter of a victim was awarded $40,000, and parents $250,000. By modern standards, the government got away with bargain-basement prices.

Although the plaintiffs were awarded rather modest sums, their attorneys declared the outcome a landmark victory. "It's the first case where a major federal activity involving radiation has been held responsible for harming civilians," said Stewart Udall. "I can't think of anywhere where the government has been held to account like this. It makes it easier for citizens to gain redress. It opens the Pandora's box that the government thought it could close."[10]

Understandably, the government wanted to shut that Pandora's box before more litigation came to light. It appealed the *Allen et al.* v. *United States* in the same federal appeals court where the *Bulloch* v. *United States* case of the sheep ranchers had been reversed.

In a matter of days, the appeals court reviewed enough of the 60,000 pages of documents and transcriptions to decide that the discretionary function exception applied in this case. The government could not be sued for its action no matter how many deaths resulted or how negligent the AEC had been. Judge Jenkins's decision was reversed. The plaintiffs' appealed to the Supreme Court, but again, as in the decision on the sheep ranchers, the court declined to hear the case.

The atomic soldiers—those who were in Hiroshima or Nagasaki after the explosions there or who participated in atomic tests—have had no more success in the courts. The main obstacle is the Feres doctrine. It is based on a 1950 Supreme Court decision that held that members of the armed forces could not sue the government for death or injuries sustained in combat. It was later interpreted to cover almost any injury suffered while in the service. In a case tried in 1979, *Jaffee* v. *United States,* a former soldier claimed that his cancer was caused by an atomic explosion. He and others had been ordered to stand at attention facing the explosion without protection or any warning of the dangers. The court decided that the government had sovereign immunity and that the military could order soldiers as it saw fit.

Veterans also faced a rather odd law that dates back to the Civil War. It prohibits veterans from spending more than $10 on legal fees on actions against the Veterans Administration to claim disability payments. A 1986 trial found that limit unconstitutional, but the Supreme Court overturned the decision. Since $10 will pay for only a few seconds of legal counsel, the law effectively denies veterans access to the legal system.

One famous case was that of Paul Cooper, a retired army sergeant. A hero in both the Korean and Vietnam conflicts, he also participated in the 1957 Smokey shot at the NTS. In 1976, he developed leukemia. His doctor identified radiation as a probable cause. The Veterans Administration, however, saw the probability as being "remote to the vanishing point."[11] Mr. Cooper applied for disability benefits three times before he finally took his case to the public. He was interviewed from his deathbed on Salt Lake City television, and that publicity led to a feature article in *Parade* magazine. The VA Board of Appeals then reversed the rejection of his third claim and agreed to pay him $820 per month. The VA did not admit that the injury was caused by his exposure to radiation, but the case did succeed in opening a can of worms. More cases, involving veterans, workers at the NTS, and downwind residents, were soon to come to court. Unfortunately, few of them would succeed.

One other law worked against atomic victims. The Warner Amendment, passed in 1984, prohibited alleged victims from suing contractors who had worked for the AEC at the test site.

Since the courts were clearly unwilling to find liability or negligence in government actions, the injured or their survivors have sought compensation through legislation. Several bills have been presented to Congress. Although congressional hearings have almost always found negligence in the military and the AEC, little has been done to move toward comprehensive compensation. In 1964, Congress approved $950,000 to compensate Marshall Islanders who developed thyroid cancer. In 1979, the House of Representatives defeated a bill to amend the law to make the United States liable for damages caused by the atomic tests. A similar bill was shot down by the Senate. (Neither bill specifically mentioned compensation.) In 1980, a bill was submitted to a house committee to make veterans eligible for injuries suffered from atomic tests. The bill never made it beyond that committee.

Several other bills died similar deaths in 1981. One of them, introduced by Senator Orrin Hatch, involved three hearings over the next year, hearings that testified to a host of grievances from citizens and veterans. Many thought the bill went too far; others felt it didn't go far enough.[12] The bill died in the Judiciary Committee. A companion bill introduced in the House also died in committee. A bill providing medical eligibility for Vietnam veterans exposed to the Agent Orange chemical included a provision to make certain illnesses of atomic veterans eligible as well. It had little effect, however. Five years later, only twenty atomic veterans had been granted medical benefits for their injuries.[13]

Another bill passed in 1984 offered a little help. It provided for a cancer screening program in the downwind communities. Again, compensation was not part of the bill.

The first true legislation on compensation was granted in the Radiation-exposed Veterans Act of 1988. It established a list of thirteen specific diseases known to be caused by radiation. The 1990 Radiation Exposure Compensation Act added two more. The listed diseases are: leukemia (other than chronic lymphocytic leukemia); cancers of the thyroid, breast, pharynx, esophagus, stomach, small intestine, pancreas, bile ducts, gall bladder, liver, salivary glands, urinary tract (including urinary bladder and kidneys); and multiple myelomas and lymphomas (except Hodgekin's disease).

Any atomic veteran suffering from one of the listed diseases is entitled to disability benefits *if* he can prove he received a dose exceeding 5 rem. He would not need to prove a link between his exposure and the disease. A death certificate, however, must list one of the diseases as the primary cause of death; no benefits are due the widow of the veteran with leukemia who dies of pneumonia.

The case of Al Maxwell illustrates the limited effectiveness of this law. Maxwell had been one of the American prisoners of war taken to Hiroshima. He saw four of his five children born with genetic abnormalities. Six unborn children, lost to miscarriages, showed signs of more serious deformities. According to his daughter, his doctor told him that his presence at Hiroshima was almost certainly the cause. He eventually developed multiple myeloma, a cancer that spreads throughout the body. When his records were sent to the VA, however, they disappeared without a trace. He claimed that when he told the VA that his experience at Hiroshima had caused his many health problems, the VA informed him that he had never been there, had never been a prisoner, that it was all a figment of his imagination, and that he was therefore not entitled to the benefits due wounded veterans.[14] When Maxwell died the VA maintained that technically his death resulted from pneumonia, which was not caused by anything in his wartime experience.[15]

Unfortunately, the law considers the list of possible ailments complete. All other ailments are excluded from consideration. Radiation, however, is strongly suspected to cause far more health problems than admitted to in the list. Veterans have testified to all sorts of problems that began shortly after exposure to radiation and continued throughout their lives. The National Association of Radiation Survivors (NARS) would like to see the list extended to include genetic defects, anemia, arthritis, cataracts, nervous disorders, sterility, nonmalignant tumors, diabetes, allergies, Addison's disease, multiple sclerosis, various cancers, and a number of other ailments.[16]

This law is also questioned because the 5 rem dose limit is of limited validity. Records were poorly kept, and all of them were underestimated since they made no allowance for internal doses. Apparently many of the records were falsified as well. The law also makes no provisions for atomic veterans' children who have suffered genetic defects. An informal survey of 700 members of the National Association of Atomic Veterans (NAAV) found 581 reports of birth or genetic defects.[17] Of the 15,000 claims applied for by veterans affected by atomic testing, only 1,400—less than 10 percent—have been granted.[18] The NAAV claims that the number is probably closer to 3 percent.

In 1990, President George Bush signed the Radiation Exposure Compensation Act. It set aside a $100 million reserve fund for downwinders who contracted one of a list of specified diseases. Individuals can receive as much as $50,000. Uranium miners can receive up to $100,000. Nonmilitary NTS workers can receive up to $75,000. Veterans can apply for benefits under this law *or* the Veterans Act of 1980. While this law seems good in intent, it, like the Veterans Act, requires proof of exposure. Mere residency in St. George, Utah, for example, is not enough. Victims must either somehow produce dosage records from the government—a difficult process that most often leads to, at best, inaccurate reports—or go to a private laboratory in hopes that chromosome analysis or whole-body exposure tests will produce reasonably accurate information. These alternatives are very expensive, however. As for those victims who have died, the only way for widows and other survivors to prove exposure would be exhume the body of the deceased and have teeth removed for analysis.

Even though virtually no one has successfully sued the government for damages caused by radiation, citizens are still trying to improve the situation. Almost 10,000 people have joined the National Association of Radiation Survivors, and thousands of veterans and veterans' widows have joined the National Association of Atomic Veterans.

The NARS claims that due to illnesses, disability, and high medical costs, 42 percent of its members live below the poverty level. About 20 percent of its members have a child with a genetic defect—far more than the 3 to 5 percent of the nation as a whole. NARS survivors live an average of only fifty-two years, twenty years less than the average.

The NARS and NAAV are trying to obtain health care and compensation for people exposed to radiation not only from nuclear tests, which it says have affected 2 million Americans, but also people who have been exposed at nuclear power plants, laboratories, weapons factories, uranium mines, or during the Persian Gulf War. The organization is demanding a more scientific basis for establishing allowable radiation exposure levels. It has a long list of cancers and illnesses that it feels should be added to the diseases covered by the Radiation Exposure Compensation Act of 1988. It believes that radiation victims have the same right to redress through the judicial system as other Americans. It is pushing the government to pass a National Nuclear Ethics Law that would make it a criminal offense for government employees or contractors to deceive citizens about potential exposure to radiation. Finally, the NARS is advocating a comprehensive worldwide test ban and an end to the development of nuclear weapons.

A NEW ATTITUDE . . . OR NOT?

The Clinton administration, which began in 1993, signaled a change in attitude toward the errors of the Atomic Energy Commission and the Department of Energy. President Clinton ordered the new secretary of the DOE, Hazel O'Leary, to put an end to the secrecy of the past and to conduct a complete investigation of AEC and DOE human radiation experiments. The Congress had ordered a similar investigation seven years earlier, under the Reagan administration, but it never got under way. O'Leary also began to release information about the size of the U.S. nuclear arsenal and stockpiles of plutonium. When she was informed of the *Albuquerque Tribune* article about the plutonium experiments conducted on unknowing humans, she said to her aide, "Let's get it out. Let's throw it on the pile."[19] She meant the pile of secrets revealed and former lies uncovered.

A *New York Times* article said, "It is no longer a secret that the Energy Department, once charged with building the world's most advanced atomic weaponry, was hardly a model of precision, tidiness, or wholesome conduct."[20]

Among the people especially happy to see the change in attitude was Keith L. Prescott, a former worker at the Nevada Test Site. He had helped dig tunnels for underground nuclear tests and contracted bone cancer in 1970. He and five other workers had brought a series of lawsuits against the government, all unsuccessful. In 1995, at the age of sixty-seven, he was the only surviving litigant, and his hopes were a bit higher than usual because of Secretary O'Leary's statement that the victims of radiation experiments should be compensated. One of his attorneys was the same Stewart Udall, former secretary of the interior, who had represented Irene Allen et al. in the famous but unsuccessful case of the downwinders. Referring to Hazel O'Leary's new attitude of openness and honesty, Udall said, "To have anyone connected with the atomic establishment speak with a moral voice is a marvelous breath of fresh air."[21]

The air was not as fresh as hoped, however. A federal judge ruled that there was insufficient evidence to prove that the six plaintiffs' cancers were caused by exposure to radiation. Saying that he doubted the case would be appealed again, attorney Udall said, "It's a sad day for the test site workers. These were good people who were sacrificed by their country and dumped on the side of the road."[22]

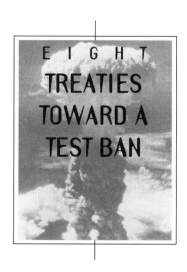

EIGHT
TREATIES TOWARD A TEST BAN

On October 31, 1958, the Soviet Union, the United States, and the United Kingdom voluntarily stopped all testing of atomic weapons. The moratorium would last almost three years. The only atomic explosions during that time were four relatively small aboveground tests conducted by France in the Sahara Desert. On August 31, 1961, the Soviet Union announced that it would resume testing. Within a week, it detonated three devices, including a 50-megaton monster that spread through the northern hemisphere. Within days, President John F. Kennedy announced that the United States would resume testing, too. At first the tests were all underground, but soon the mushroom clouds began rising over Nevada again. The underground tests did not do such a good job of preventing fallout anyway. Of the three underground tests in the Hardtack II series, only one was fully contained. The worst of that series, Shot Sedan, in 1963—a thermonuclear device buried 635 feet deep (almost 200 m)—blew open a crater 1,200 feet (about 365 m) across and 320 feet (almost 100 m) deep and heaved a tremendous amount of radioactive materials into the air.

On August 5, 1963, the United States, the Soviet Union, and the United Kingdom signed the Limited · Nuclear Test Ban Treaty, which prohibited nuclear explosions of any size anywhere in the atmosphere, outer space, or ocean. In other words, test would have to be done underground. And an underground test would be legal only if no radioactive debris resulted outside the territorial limits of the country that conducted the test. With the signing of that treaty, fallout became a question not only of safety but of international law. Unlike U.S. law, international law is not skewed in favor of the U.S. government. Most tests, therefore, have been conducted much more deeply underground than before, when tests were conducted as near to the surface as possible.[1]

The test ban held. The three signatories to the treaty conducted all tests underground, albeit with considerable leakage of radiation into the atmosphere. France and China, however, continued atmospheric tests for several years. France detonated forty-one more bombs in the atmosphere, the last in 1974. China detonated twenty-three, the last in 1980. India joined in nuclear club with an underground explosion in 1974.[2] Except for the French and Chinese tests and the approximately forty incidents in which U.S. underground tests vented into the atmosphere (and undoubtedly some in the Soviet Union), our planet's air has not been further contaminated by atomic blasts.

The Soviet Union was the first nuclear power to renounce all testing; its last atomic detonation was on October 24, 1990. On November 26, 1991, the United Kingdom conducted its last test. The United States was last of the three Limited Test Ban signers to join the moratorium on all tests, conducting its last test on September 23, 1992. The previous day, President George Bush had signed a law allowing only fifteen tests between then and September 30, 1996, after which there would be no more testing at all.

In 1995, however, France announced a series of underground tests that was to begin in September of that year and end in May of 1996. The tests were to take place in French Polynesia in the South Pacific.[3] Thousands of demonstrators marched in Paris to protest and threatened larger demonstrations on August 6 and 9, the fiftieth anniversary of the bombings of Hiroshima and Nagasaki.[4] Australia and New Zealand protested the plan. The Greenpeace ship *Rainbow Warrior II*—which replaced its predecessor, which the French had sunk in 1985—headed for the target site in hope of stopping, stalling, or at least protesting the first test. When French commandos seized the ship, protest spread around the world, but France went ahead with the tests. Although the protests had no effect on French policy, Nobel laureate Joseph Rotblat, who had worked toward abolition of all nuclear weapons, saw some good in them. He said the global reaction to the tests practically guaranteed the signing of a comprehensive test ban in 1996.[5]

There is hope that the world has seen or soon will see its last nuclear explosion. The Nuclear Nonproliferation Treaty (NPT) brought almost all nonnuclear powers to an agreement not to develop, possess, or test atomic weapons. However, it did not prohibit the declared nuclear powers from testing their weapons. Since the NPT went into force in 1970, it has been largely effective in preventing the spread of atomic weapons, and in 1995, 170 nations agreed to continue the terms of the treaty indefinitely. The current declared nuclear powers—the United States, Russia, the United Kingdom, France, and China—have agreed to reduce the number of their weapons and strive to eliminate all of them, though they have been under worldwide criticism for failing to move fast enough.[6] It is hoped that the nations that have nuclear weapons but have not declared them—Israel, Pakistan, and India, none of which have signed the NPT—will refrain from testing or using those weapons. Three former Soviet republics have agreed to destroy or hand over to Russia the atomic weapons that were left on their territory when the Soviet Union broke up in 1991.

The danger of nuclear proliferation is still with us. Nondemocratic nations such as Iraq, Iran, and North Korea are known to have been seeking the equipment and ingredients needed to build an atomic bomb.[7] It is also possible that terrorists, who are obviously not subject to international treaties and are generally notorious for their reckless behavior, may some day get hold of an atomic weapon.[8] Modern technology has made it possible for a nation or organization to develop a nuclear weapon without testing it. It can build a single bomb and be confident that it will explode when triggered.[9]

The world now faces the possibility of a Comprehensive Test Ban (CTB). Most of the countries of the world are hoping to agree to such a ban in 1996. There is controversy, however. The United States, Russia, the United Kingdom, and France all want to allow the testing of very small devices. The tests would be to ensure the safety of the other atomic weapons in their arsenals. The United States would like to see a maximum yield of just 4 pounds (1.8 kg) of TNT, a minuscule explosion by atomic standards. The United Kingdom wants to conduct tests that yield up to a few hundred pounds. France says 200 pounds (about 90 kg) would suffice. Russia thinks tens of tons would be necessary.[10]

The miniature atomic explosions are called hydronuclear detonations. The prefix *hydro* refers to certain parts of the bomb that liquefy during the explosion process. Much of the fuel consists of isotopes that do not undergo chain reaction.[11]

Other countries feel that a Comprehensive Test Ban should be truly comprehensive, that is, including *all* bombs of *all* sizes. The concerns go beyond the general fear of radiation and loathing of atomic weapons. There is worry that tests of such small bombs might encourage nonnuclear countries to develop small weapons or use hydronuclear technology secretly. This will be a major controversy until it comes time to agree on a CTB treaty. Dr. Frank von Hippel, a physicist at Princeton University and adviser to the White House, said that one way to clear up the controversy would be to allow only a test with a yield of zero.[12]

Such a test might be possible. As the Clinton administration faced the political wisdom of a CTB and the conflicting need to test current weapons, the construction of a special facility was proposed. It would be able to focus 192 lasers on a tiny pellet of supercold hydrogen fuel for one one-billionth of a second, touching off a tiny fusion reaction. The price tag, $18 billion, however, made it doubtful that the facility would ever be built.[13] It seemed a lot cheaper just to stop testing altogether. To most people of the world, it seemed about time.

GLOSSARY

AEC - the U.S. Atomic Energy Commission, founded in 1946 and dissolved in 1974. During its tenure, the AEC oversaw, regulated, and controlled all activities involving radioactive materials, including weapons design, production and testing, nuclear power plants, nuclear medicine, the mining of uranium, and nuclear waste disposal.

alpha radiation - atomic radiation consisting of an alpha particle, that is, two protons and two neutrons. Relatively heavy and slow, alpha particles do not go far and cannot penetrate a sheet of paper or human skin. Inside the human body, however, they can cause severe damage to adjacent tissue.

atomic bomb - an explosive device designed to set off an uncontrolled fission chain reaction in a critical mass of nuclear fuel.

becquerel - a unit of measurement of atomic decay, replacing the old term, *curie*. One becquerel equals one unit of decay per second. One curie equals 37,000 million becquerels.

beta radiation - atomic radiation consisting of a beta particle, that is, the particle that is emitted when a neutron converts to a proton. Beta particles are lighter and faster than alpha particles; therefore, they can travel farther and penetrate the human body. They are a dangerous external source of radiation, though internally they are less dangerous than alpha radiation.

cesium-137 (C-137) - a radioactive isotope of cesium.

chain reaction, nuclear - the process in which atoms of a radioactive isotope break up, releasing neutrons, which in turn break up more atoms, releasing atomic energy.

critical mass - the amount of radioactive material needed to start a nuclear chain reaction.

CTB - Comprehensive Test Ban.

curie - a unit of measurement of the rate of the atomic decay that is radiation. *See* becquerel.

DOD - the U.S. Department of Defense.

DOE - the U.S. Department of Energy, established in 1977.

epidimologist - one who deals with the incidence and control of disease in a population.

fallout - the radioactive particles that fall from radioactive clouds, especially those of atomic explosions.

fission - the nuclear chain reaction that releases energy by splitting atoms into smaller atoms.

fusion - the combining of atoms to produce a more massive atom, releasing energy in the process; the explosive process of a hydrogen bomb.

gamma radiation - atomic radiation consisting of a wave of energy, not unlike X rays. They can shoot right through the human body and even penetrate several inches of metal or concrete. Traveling far and fast from the radionuclide that emits them, gamma rays are a dangerous external radiation.

gray - a modern unit of measurement of absorbed dose of radiation, replacing the rad. One gray equals 100 rad.

ground zero - the point on the surface of the earth directly below an atomic explosion.

hydrogen bomb - an atomic weapon in which a fission explosion provides the heat and energy needed to cause the nuclear fusion of hydrogen atoms, releasing a tremendous amount of energy.

hydronuclear detonation - a new technology that allows a very small amount of nuclear fuel to produce a very small nuclear explosion. The process is used to test nuclear weapons fuel and designs.

iodine-131 (I-131) - a radioactive isotope of iodine, dangerous for its tendency to accumulate in the thyroid gland.

kiloton (kt) - the explosive power of 1,000 tons of TNT.

kt - *see* kiloton.

megaton (mt) - the explosive power of 1,000,000 (1 million) tons of TNT.

mt - *see* megaton.

neutron radiation - neutrons released during fission, a dangerous source of external radiation.

neutron - one of the two large particles in the nucleus of an atom. It has a no electric charge. Nuclear chain reactions are caused when neutrons released from atoms break up other atoms, releasing energy. Neutrons are also an especially dangerous form of radiation occurring at a nuclear explosion.

NPT - Nuclear Nonproliferation Treaty.

nuclear device - an atomic weapon.

nuclear fuel - the mass of radioactive isotopes used to power a nuclear bomb or a nuclear power plant. A bomb normally uses uranium-238 or plutonium-239.

plutonium - an extremely poisonous radioactive element that occurs only rarely in nature. It is normally created by converting uranium. The plutonium-239 isotope is a very efficient atomic bomb fuel. Two other isotopes are plutonium-240 and plutonium-241.

rad - radiation absorbed dose, a unit of measurement of how much nuclear radiation is actually absorbed by living tissue. A rad is *approximately* equal to a roentgen. The rad has been replaced by a unit called the gray. One gray equals 100 rad.

radioisotope - a radioactive isotope of an element, e.g., plutonium-239, iodine-131, cesium-137, uranium-235.

radionuclide - a radioactive atom.

rainout - radioactive particles (fallout) falling with rain.

rem - roentgen equivalent in man, a unit of measurement of the extent to which a given type of radiation affects a given organ or type of human tissue. One rem is often approximately equal to 1 rad, but in the case of more dangerous forms of radiation—alpha and neutron radiation, for example—1 rad may equal 10 or 20 rem, respectively. The rem unit has been replaced by the sievert, with 1 sievert equal to 100 rem.

roentgen - a unit for measuring the strength of radiation in the air.

sievert - a unit of measurement of the effect of radiation on human tissue. The sievert replaces the rem unit, with 1 sievert equal to 100 rem.

strontium-90 (Sr-90) - a radioactive isotope that is chemically similar to calcium.

test shot - an atomic explosion conducted for experimental purposes.

thermonuclear weapon - a fusion bomb, commonly referred to as a hydrogen bomb. A thermonuclear-boosted fission weapon has a small amount of fusion fuel at its core, which, upon detonation, boosts the yield of the fission explosion.

uranium - a radioactive element occurring in nature and that can be purified into uranium-235 and uranium-238, the latter being a common fuel of atomic weapons. Uranium can be processed into plutonium through atomic reaction.

venting - the accidental escape of radiation from an underground nuclear test.

SUGGESTED READING

Advisory Committee on Human Radiation Experiments—Final Report. Washington, DC: U.S. Government Printing Office, October 1995. Also available as an Executive Summary.

American Ground Zero: The Secret Nuclear War, by Carole Gallagher. Cambridge, MA: MIT Press, 1993.

Bombs in the Backyard: Atomic Testing and American Politics, by A. Constandina Titus. Reno: University of Nevada Press, 1986.

Bulletin of the Atomic Scientists, a monthly magazine published in Chicago.

Day of Two Suns: U.S. Nuclear Testing and the Pacific Islanders, by Jane Dibblin. New York: New Amsterdam, 1988.

Deadly Deceit, by Jay M. Gould and Benjamin Goldman. New York: Four Walls Eight Windows, 1991.

Elements of Controversy: The Atomic Energy Commission and Radiation Safety in Nuclear Weapons Testing, by Barton C. Hacker. Los Angeles: University of California Press, 1994.

Fallout: An American Nuclear Tragedy, by Philip L. Fradkin. Tucson: University of Arizona Press, 1989.

The Forgotton Guinea Pigs: A Report on Health Effects of Low-Level Radiation Sustained As a Result of the Nuclear Weapons Testing Program Conducted by the United States Government, Committee on Interstate and Foreign Commerce, United States House of Representatives, Subcommittee on Oversight and Investigations, 1993.

The Greenpeace Book of the Nuclear Age: The Hidden History, the Human Cost, by John May. New York: Pantheon Books, 1989.

In the Shadow of the Cloud: Photographs and Histories of America's Atomic Bomb Veterans, by Jim Lerager. Golden, CO: Fulcrum, 1988.

Justice Downwind: America's Atomic Testing Program in the 1950s, by Howard Ball. New York: Oxford University Press, 1986.

Nuclear Landscapes, by Peter Goin. Baltimore: Johns Hopkins University Press, 1991.

"The Plutonium Experiment" by Eileen Welsome. Reprint from *The Albuquerque [NM] Tribune,* November 15, 1993.

Proliferation of Weapons of Mass Destruction: Assessing the Risks, Office of Technology Assessment, United States Congress, Washington, DC, 1993.

Time Bomb, by Corinne Brown and Robert Monroe. New York: William Morrow, 1981.

Under the Cloud: The Decades of Nuclear Testing, by Richard L. Miller. New York: The Free Press, 1986.

SOURCE NOTES

INTRODUCTION

1 "Known Nuclear Tests Worldwide, 1945–94," *Bulletin of the Atomic Scientists*, May/June 1995, pp. 70–71.

2 Jay M. Gould and Benjamin Goldman, *Deadly Deceit,* New York: Four Walls Eight Windows, 1991, p. 99.

3 Carole Gallagher, *American Ground Zero: The Secret Nuclear War,* Cambridge, MA: MIT Press, 1993, p. 288.

4 Richard L. Miller, *Under the Cloud: The Decades of Nuclear Testing,* New York: The Free Press, 1986, p. 62

5 Jane Dibblin, *Day of Two Suns: U.S. Nuclear Testing and the Pacific Islanders,* New York: New Amsterdam, 1988.

6 Eileen Welsome, "The Plutonium Experiment," [a reprint from] *The Albuquerque Tribune,* November 15, 1993.

7 Philip L. Fradkin, *Fallout: An American Nuclear Tragedy,* Tucson: The University of Arizona Press, 1989, p. 113.

CHAPTER ONE

1 William J. Broad, "Making Nuclear Arms Is Easier Than It Looks, New Study Says," *The New York Times,* August 21, 1994, p. 1.

2 *Health Effects of Exposure to Low Levels of Ionizing Radiation: BIER V,* National Research Council, Washington, DC: National Academy Press, 1990, p. 19.

3 *Ibid.,* pp. 46–49.

4 *The Forgotton Guinea Pigs: A Report on Health Effects of Low-Level Radiation Sustained As a Result of the Nuclear Weapons*

Testing Program Conducted by the United States Government, a report prepared for the Committee on Interstate and Foreign Commerce, United States House of Representatives, Subcommittee on Oversight and Investigations, August 1980, p. 32.

5 John May, *The Greenpeace Book of the Nuclear Age: The Hidden History, the Human Cost,* New York: Pantheon Books, 1989, pp. 34-35.

CHAPTER TWO

1 Barton C. Hacker, *The Dragon's Tail: Radiation Safety in the Manhattan Project, 1942–1946,* Berkeley: University of California Press, 1987, p. 113.

2 Donald I. Collins, "Pictures from the Past: Journeys into Health Physics in the Manhattan Project and Other Diverse Places," in *Health Physics: A Backward Glance,* ed. Ronald Kathleen and Paul Ziemer, New York: Pergamon Press, 1980.

3 A. Constandina Titus, *Bombs in the Backyard: Atomic Testing and American Politics,* Reno: University of Nevada Press, 1986, p. 21.

4 Ibid, p. 27.

5 Hacker, p. 121.

6 Richard L. Miller, *Under the Cloud: The Decades of Nuclear Testing,* New York: The Free Press, 1986, p. 78, citing *Los Angeles Times,* August 2, 1946.

7 *Bulletin of the Atomic Scientists,* May/June 1994, p. 26, quoting from *Operation Crossroads: The Atomic Tests at Bikini Atoll,* by Jonathan M. Weisgall, Naval Institute Press, 1994.

8 Mike Moore, "The Able-Baker-Where's-Charlie Follies," *Bulletin of the Atomic Scientists,* May/June 1994, pp. 26–27.

9 Moore, *op. cit.,* p. 29.

10 Miller, p. 62.

11 Howard Ball, *Justice Downwind; America's Atomic Testing Program in the 1950s,* New York: Oxford, 1986, p. 16.

CHAPTER THREE

1 Patrick Hughes and David Konigsberg, "Grim Legacy of Nuclear Testing," *The New York Times Magazine,* April 2, 1979, p. 34.

2 Carole Gallagher, *American Ground Zero: The Secret Nuclear War,* Cambridge, MA: MIT Press, 1993, p. xxiii.

3 Howard Ball, *Justice Downwind; America's Atomic Testing Program in the 1950s,* New York: Oxford, 1986, p. 85.

4 Philip J. Hilts, "Fallout Risks Near Atom Tests Were Known, Documents Show," *The New York Times*, March 15, 1995, p. 22.

5 *Ibid.*, p. 22.

6 *Las Vegas Review Journal,* January 28, 1984, p. 1C.

7 Ball, p. 35.

8 Ball, p. 60, a repoduction of government handbill dated January 11, 1951.

9 Ball, p. 68.

10 Hilts, p. 23.

11 Ball, p. 43.

12 Philip L. Fradkin, *Fallout: An American Nuclear Tragedy*, Tucson: The University of Arizona Press, 1989, p. 113.

13 Ball, pp. 81–82.

14 Barton C. Hacker, *Elements of Controversy: The Atomic Energy Commission and Radiation Safety in Nuclear Weapons Testing,* Los Angeles: University of California Press, p. 177.

15 Fradkin, *op. cit.,* p. 113.

16 *Ibid.*, p. 44.

17 Richard L. Miller, *Under the Cloud: The Decades of Nuclear Testing,* New York: The Free Press, 1986, p. 8.

18 Other shots left other hot spots. In the Tumbler-Snapper series, Shot George left 1,400,000 disintegrations per square foot per minute in Pocatello, ID, Shot How raised radiation in Great Falls, MT, to 5,900,000 disintegrations per minute. After Shot Annie in the Upshot-Knothole series, the number was 1,900,000 in Knoxville, TN, and 1,000,000 in Dallas, TX. The number after Shot Encore was 1,200,000 in Weilliston, ND and 570,000 in Bermuda. After Shot Harry, disintegrations per minute per square foot were at 11,00,000 in Grand Junction, CO, 7,800,000 in Albuquerque, NM, 2,000,000 in Raton, NM, 1,600,000 in Amarillo TX, 1,500,000 in Des Moines, IA, 8,400 in Bermuda, 1,200 in Seattle, WA. For more details, see Richard L. Miller, p. 8

19 Miller, p. 164.

20 Warren E. Leary, "In the 1950's, U.S. Collected Human Tissue to Monitor Atomic Tests," *The New York Times*, June 21, 1995, p. B-8.

21 Hacker, p. 231.

22 John May, *The Greenpeace Book of the Nuclear Age: The Hidden History, the Human Cost,* New York: Pantheon Books, 1989, pp. 92–99.

23 *Ibid.*, p. 132.

24 *Ibid.*, p. 248

25 Dibblin, *op. cit.*, p. 208.

26 "France Attacks European Allies Over Nuclear Vote in the U.N.," Reuters, printed in *The New York Times,* December 14, 1995, p. A-5.

CHAPTER FOUR

1 A. Constandina Titus, *Bombs in the Backyard: Atomic Testing and American Politics,* Reno: University of Nevada Press, 1986, p. 59.

2 Jim Lerager, *In the Shadow of the Cloud: Photographs and Histories of America's Atomic Bomb Veterans,* Golden, CO: Fulcrum, 1988, p. 107.

3 Howard Ball, *Justice Downwind: America's Atomic Testing Program in the 1950s,* New York: Oxford, 1986, p. 31.

4 Richard L. Miller, *Under the Cloud: The Decades of Nuclear Testing,* New York: The Free Press, 1986, pp. 149–68.

5 Thomas H. Saffer and Orville E. Kelly, *Countdown Zero,* New York: G. P. Putnam's Sons, 1982, p. 47.

6 Carole Gallagher, *American Ground Zero: The Secret Nuclear War,* Cambridge, MA: MIT Press, 1993, p. 62, citing *Washington Law Review,* 65, no. 2, April 1990.

7 Gallagher, *op. cit.,* p. 63.

8 UPI story reported in *The New York Times,* February 8, 1982, p. A-14.

9 Ball, p. 85.

10 *Ibid.,* p. 11.

11 "National Association of Radiation Survivors Summary of Issues and Demands" NARS, Live Oak, CA.

12 Gallagher, *op. cit.,* p. 21

13 *Ibid.,* p. 17.

14 Lerager, *op. cit.,* p. 26.

15 *Ibid.,* p. 54.

16 *Ibid.,* p. 46.

17 *Ibid.,* p. 48.

CHAPTER FIVE

1 *Desert News,* March 26, 1953, p. 15A.

2 *Atomic Tests in Nevada,* United States Atomic Energy Commission, March 1957.

3 A. Constandina Titus, *Bombs in the Backyard: Atomic Testing and American Politics,* Reno: University of Nevada Press, 1986, p. 86.

4 Daniel Lang, "Blackjack and Flashes," *The New Yorker,* Sept. 20, 1952, p. 109.

5 *Ibid.,* p. 101.

6 *Las Vegas Review-Journal,* May 24, 1953, p. 1.

7 *Las Vegas Review-Journal,* February 18, 1955, p. 1.

8 *The Forgotton Guinea Pigs,* p. vii.

9 Titus, *op. cit.,* p. 65.

10 Barton C. Hacker, *Elements of Controversy: The Atomic Energy Commission and Radiation Safety in Nuclear Weapons Testing,* Los Angeles: University of California Press, 1994, p. 164.

11 *Ibid.,* p. 110.

12 *Ibid.,* p. 3.

13 *Ibid.,* p. 112

14 "AEC Denies Rays Killed Utah Sheep," *The New York Times,* January 17, 1954, p. 46.

15 Howard Ball, *Justice Downwind: America's Atomic Testing Program in the 1950s,* New York: Oxford, 1986, p. 206.

16 *Ibid.,* p. 207

17 *Ibid.,* p. viii

18 *Ibid.,* p. 8.

19 *Ibid.,* p. 2.

20 *Government Liability for Atomic Weapons Testing Program,* Hearing Before the Committee on the Judiciary, United States Senate, June 27, 1986, p. 182.

CHAPTER SIX

1 Carole Gallagher, *American Ground Zero: The Secret Nuclear War,* Cambridge, MA: MIT Press, 1993, p. 146.

2 Richard L. Miller, *Under the Cloud: The Decades of Nuclear Testing,* New York: The Free Press, 1986, p. 382.

3 "Nuclear Victims" *Life,* June 1980, p. 36.

4 Norman Soloman and Harvey Wasserman, "We All Live Downwind," *Environmental Action,* April 1993, p. 16.

5 *Ibid.,* p. 18.

6 *The Forgotton Guinea Pigs: A Report on Health Effects of Low-Level Radiation Sustained As a Result of the Nuclear Weapons Testing Program Conducted by the United States Government,* a report prepared for the Committee on Interstate and Foreign Commerce, United States House of Representatives, Subcommittee on Oversight and Investigations, August 1980, p. 14.

7 Miller, *op. cit.,* pp. 186–87.

8 Paul Jacobs, "Precautions Are Being Taken by Those Who Know," *The Atlantic,* February 1971, p. 45ff.

9 Dr. Linus Pauling, "How Dangerous Is Radioactive Fallout?" *Foreign Policy Bulletin,* June 15, 1957, p. 149.

10 Dr. Linus Pauling, *No More War,* New York: Dodd Mead, 1958.

11 A. Constandina Titus, *Bombs in the Backyard: Atomic Testing and American Politics,* Reno: University of Nevada Press, 1986, p. 98.

12 Jay M. Gould and Benjamin Goldman, *Deadly Deceit,* New York: Four Walls Eight Windows, 1991, p. 99.

13 Miller, *op. cit.,* pp. 338–39.

14 Gould and Goldman, p. 98.

15 Gallagher, *op. cit.,* pp. 325–26.

16 Corinne Brown and Robert Monroe, *Time Bomb,* New York: William Morrow, 1981, p. 142.

17 Gallagher, *op. cit.,* pp. 325–33.

18 Ernest Sternglass, "Infant Mortality and Nuclear Tests," *Bulletin of the Atomic Scientists,* April 1969, p. 19.

19 Ernest J. Sternglass, "The Death of All Children," *Esquire,* September 1969, p. 120.

20 Ball, *op. cit.,* p. 108.

21 *The Forgotton Guinea Pigs,* p. 20.

22 *The Forgotton Guinea Pigs,* p. 15.

23 Dr. Joseph Lyons, *Health Effects of Radiation Exposure,* Hearing before the Committee on Labor and Human Resources, United States Senate, February 8, 1990, pp. 15–16.

24 There is also evidence that the AEC specifically avoided analyzing milk and preventing others from doing so. Dr. John Willard, Sr., who had worked on the Manhattan project, was an AEC consultant living in North Dakota during the Diablo shot of 1957. When a friend noticed high readings on her Geiger counter after a heavy rain, he alerted civil defense officials. They declared the milk of several states contaminated and warned farmers that their hay was contaminated. Two days later, FBI agents took him to the Nevada Test Site, where he was scolded for trying to start public panic. AEC officials threatened to have him imprisoned for treason. Gallagher, *op. cit.,* pp. 288–89.

35 Harold Knapp, "Observed Relationships Between Deposition Level of Fresh Fission products from Nevada and Resulting Levels of I–131 in Fresh Milk," AEC report, March 1, 1963, p. 1.

26 Miller, *op. cit.,* p. 364.

27 *The Forgotton Guinea Pigs,* p. 17.

28 *Ibid.*, p. 17.

29 *Ibid.*, p. 17.

30 Joseph L. Lyons et al. "Childhood Leukemias Associated with Fallout from Nuclear Testing," *New England Journal of Medicine*, February 22, 1979, p. 397.

31 Charles E. Land, "Childhood Leukemia and the Nevada Tests," *Science*, January 13, 1984, p. 139.

32 Glyn G. Caldwell, "Leukemia Among Participants in Military Maneuvers at a Nuclear Bomb Test," *Journal of the American Medical Association*, October 3, 1980, pp. 1575–78.

33 V. P. Bond and L. D. Hamilton, "Leukemia in the Nevada Smokey Bomb Test," *Journal of the American Medical Association*, October 3, 1980, p. 1610.

34 Glyn G. Caldwell et al., "Mortality and Cancer Frequency Among Nuclear Test (Smokey) Participants," *Journal of the American Medical Association*, August 5, 1983, pp. 620–24.

35 Harold L. Beck and Philip W. Krey, "Radiation Exposures in Utah from the Nevada Nuclear Tests, *Science*, April 1, 1983, pp. 18–24.

36 Carl J. Johnson, M.D., "Cancer Incidence in an Area of Radioactive Fallout Downwind from the Nevada Test Site," *Journal of the American Medical Association,* January 13, 1984, p. 1102.

37 Dr. Joseph Lyons, *Health Effects of Radiation Exposure*, Hearing Before the Committee on Labor and Human Resources, United States Senate, February 8, 1990, p. 21.

38 *Ibid.*, p. 224.

39 Gould and Goldman, pp. 95–109.

40 S. Shapiro, E. R. Schlesinger, and R. E. I. Nesbitt, *Infant, Perinatal, Maternal and Childhood Maternity in the United States*, Cambridge, MA: Harvard University Press, 1968, p. 107.

41 K. S. Lee et al. "Neonatal Mortality: Analysis of Recent Improvement in the U.S.," *American Journal of Public Health*, vol. 70, 1980, p. 17.

42 Eileen Welsome, "The Plutonium Experiment," [a reprint from] *The Albuquerque Tribune*, November 15, 1993, p. 24.

43 Philip J. Hilts, "Panel Finds Wide Debate in 40s on the Ethics of Radiation Tests," *The New York Times*, October 11, 1994, p. A-3.

44 *Advisory Committee on Human Radiation Experiments—Final Report*, October 1995, U.S. Government Printing Office.

45 Philip J. Hilts, "Panels Urges U.S. to Apologize for Radiation Testing and Pay Damages," *The New York Times*, October 3, 1995, p. A-19.

46 H. Joseg Hebert, "Panel Urges Government to Pay Radiation Experiment Victims," Associated Press, October 3, 1995.

CHAPTER SEVEN

1 A. Constandina Titus, *Bombs in the Backyard: Atomic Testing and American Politics*, Reno: University of Nevada Press, 1986, p. 110.

2 *The Forgotton Guinea Pigs: A Report on Health Effects of Low-Level Radiation Sustained As a Result of the Nuclear Weapons Testing Program Conducted by the United States Government*, a report prepared for the Committee on Interstate and Foreign Commerce, United States House of Representatives, Subcommittee on Oversight and Investigations, August 1980, p. 10.

3 Titus, *op. cit.*, pp. 3–13.

4 *Ibid.*, p. 13.

5 Ball, *op. cit.*, p. 207, citing *Bulloch* v. *United States.*

6 *Ibid.*, p. 147.

7 Ball, *op. cit.*, p. 152.

8 *Ibid.*, p. 153.

9 Philip L. Fradkin, *Fallout: An American Nuclear Tragedy*, Tucson: The University of Arizona Press, 1989, p. 229.

10 Iver Peterson, "U.S. Ruled Negligent in A-Tests Followed by Nine Cancer Deaths," *The New York Times*, May 11, 1984, p. 1. (The article refered to nine deaths because one successful plaintiff died after the trial ended.)

11 Titus, *op. cit.*, p. 107.

12 *Ibid.*, p. 139.

13 *Ibid.*, p. 137.

14 Carole Gallagher, *American Ground Zero: The Secret Nuclear War*, Cambridge, MA: MIT Press, 1993, pp. 103–4.

15 Jim Lerager, *In the Shadow of the Cloud: Photographs and Histories of America's Atomic Bomb Veterans*, Golden, CO: Fulcrum, 1988, p. 42.

16 "National Association of Radiation Survivors Summary of Issues and Demands," NARS, P.O. Box 278, Live Oaks, CA 95953.

17 Mary Manning, "Atomic Vets Battle Time," *Bulletin of the Atomic Scientists*, January/February 1995, p. 60.

18 *Ibid.*, p. 60.

19 Eileen Welsome, "The Plutonium Experiment," [a reprint from] *The Albuquerque Tribune*, November 15, 1993.

20 Keith Schneider, "Energy Chief in Spotlight As She Uncovers the Past," *The New York Times*, January 6, 1994, p. A-1.

21 Michael Janofsky, "After Years of Suing U.S., Hope for A-Bomb Worker," *The New York Times,* January 6, 1995, p. 20.

22 Associated Press, "Lawsuit by Nuclear Test Site Workers Fails," reported in *The New York Times*, July 23, 1995, p. 26.

CHAPTER EIGHT

1 Barton C. Hacker, *Elements of Controversy: The Atomic Energy Commission and Radiation Safety in Nuclear Weapons Testing*, Los Angeles: University of California Press, 1994, p. 231.
2 "Known Nuclear Tests Worldwide, 1945–1994," *Bulletin of the Atomic Scientists*, May/June 1995, p. 71.
3 Craig R. Whitney, "France Planning Nuclear Tests Despite Opposition, Chirac Says," *The New York Times*, June 14, 1995, p. A-2.
4 Associated Press report, June 20, 1995.
5 "Nobel Winner Says Test Ban Seems Nearer," *The New York Times*, November 12, 1995, p. A-8.
6 Barbara Crossette, "Gore, at U.N., Says Nuclear Powers Are Fair on Weapons Treaty," *The New York Times*, April 20, 1995, p. A-14.
7 Leonard Spector, "Strategic Warning and New Nuclear States," *Director's Series on Proliferation*, National Technical Information Service, Washington, D.C., August 12, 1994, pp. 1–5.
8 *U.S. Policy Toward Rogue Regimes*, Hearings Before the Subcommittee on International Security, International Organizations and Human Rights of the Committee on Foreign Affairs, House of Representatives, July 28 and September 14, 1993, pp. 35–36.
9 *Proliferation of Weapons of Mass Destruction: Assessing the Risks*, Office of Technology Asssessment, United States Congress, Washington, DC, p. 35.
10 William J. Broad, "Atom Powers Want to Test Despite Treaty," *The New York Times*, March 29, 1995, p. A-6.
11 *Ibid.*, p. A-6.
12 *Ibid.*, p. A-6.
13 "U.S. to Build Laser to Make Nuclear Fire," *The New York Times*, October 21, 1994, p. A-1.

INDEX

Able test, 30–31, 60
Agent Orange, 100
Alamogordo, NM, test at, 23–25
Albuquerque Tribune, 84–86, 103
Allen, Irene, 93, 104
Allen et al v. United States, 93–97
Alpha radiation, 16
Amchitka Island, 36
Atomic bomb (A-bomb), 12–13
    and Cold War, 22–34
Atomic Energy Act of 1946, 29
Atomic Energy Commission (AEC),
    9, 10, 29, 35, 37, 42–43, 45–
    46, 62, 63–64, 66–67, 68, 70,
    74, 78, 79, 88–104
Atomic explosions, open-air, 7
Atomic testing, 10, 51–61, 107
Atomic veterans, 26–29, 61, 98,
    100
Atomic warfare, simulated, 51–57
Atomic weapons, 13–14
Auckland Harbor, 50
Australia, 48, 107

Baker test, 31–33, 60
Baneberry accident, 59

Becquerel, 17
Beryllium, 48
Beta radiation, 16
Bikini Atoll, 30, 60
Bismuth, 17
Black, Marjorie, 43–44
Brower, Stephen, 68–69
Bulloch v. United States, 97–98
Bullock, Kern, 65–66
Bunkerville, NV, 71
Butrico, Frank, 40, 41, 44–45, 95

Caldwell, Glyn, 80–81
Cancer, 7, 17, 18, 19, 20, 71–82,
    100, 101
Carter, Robert, 55–56
Castle series, 60
Cataracts, 7, 101
Cedar City, UT, 40, 71
Centers for Disease Control, 80
Central Intelligence Agency, 87
Cesium, 8, 81
Chain reaction, 12–13
Charlie test, 30, 33
Chemical explosion, 13
China, 33, 48, 106, 107

Christensen, Sherman, 68, 92
Christmas Island, 48, 49
Clinton, Bill, 86, 87, 103
Cold War, and bomb, 22–34
Compensation, 8, 57, 88, 96–97, 99
Comprehensive Test Ban (CTB), 108, 109
Contamination, 8, 9, 26–29, 32
Cooper, Paul, 43, 80, 98–99
Cousteau, Jacques, 49
Critical mass, 12–13
Crossroads tests, 30–33
Curie, Marie, 26–27

Deadly Deceit (Gould/Goldman), 82–83
Death(s), from nuclear tests, 7, 8, 20, 25–26
Defense Nuclear Agency, 55
Department of Defense (DOD), 53–54, 87
Department of Energy (DOE), 20, 85–87, 90, 103
Department of Veterans Affairs, 87
Desert News, 41, 62
Detonation, and altitude, 13
DNA, effect of radiation on, 17–18
Dosage, inaccurate records of, 101
Dose equivalent, 17
Downwinders, 36, 72, 102

Eisenhower, Dwight D., 63–64
Energy Research and Development Commission (ERDC), 90
Eniwetok Island, 60
Esquire magazine, 74, 75

Fallout, 8, 9, 15, 106
Federal Tort Claims Act (FTCA), 89, 94
Feres doctrine, 98
Fission bomb, 12–13

Forgotten Guinea Pigs, The, 91–93
France, 46, 48, 49, 105, 106, 107, 108
Freedom of Information Act, 77, 86, 90
Fudge, Ben, 60–61
Fusion bomb, 13

Geiger counter, 39, 43, 45, 62
Genetic defects, 7, 17–18, 20, 101–2
Gofman, John, 73–74
Goldman, Benjamin A., 82–83
Gould, Jay M., 82–83
Greenpeace, 49–50, 107
Groves, Leslie, 22, 24, 27, 29, 33

Hardtack II series, 105
Hiroshima, 20–21, 25, 26–29, 97, 100, 101, 107
Hot spots, 45
Human injury, trial on, 93–97
Hydrogen bomb (H-bomb), 13, 60
Hydronuclear detonations, 108–9

Immunological weakness, as caused by radiation, 7
India, 106, 108
Infant mortality, 45, 74–75, 82–83
Internal dose, 70, 75–76, 85, 91
International Commission on Radiological Protection, 20
International testing, 48–50
Iodine-131, 8, 76, 77
Isotope, defined, 4

Jackson, Henry "Scoop," 64
Jaffee v. United States, 98
Japan, 22–26
    See also Hiroshima; Nagasaki
Jenkins, Bruce, 94, 96
Johnson, Carl, 81, 82

Joint Committee on Atomic Energy (JCAE), 64, 74

Kennedy, John F., 46, 105
Knapp, Harold, 41, 69–70, 75
  on iodine-131, 77, 78–79

Laird, Martha, 43, 72
Land, Charles E., 79–80
Las Vegas, NV, 38, 57, 64
Leukemia, 7, 18, 19–20, 25, 26–27, 45, 60, 71, 79–81, 82
Limited Nuclear Test Ban Treaty, 106
Livermore Laboratories, 74
Lymphona, 60, 82
Lyons, Joseph, 78, 79–80, 82, 94–95

Mackelprang, Elma, 40
Manhattan Project, 22
Marshall Islanders, 99
Marshall Islands, 8, 29–33, 35, 60–61
Maxwell, Al, 26, 100–101
Mental retardation, 7, 73–74
Merron, Robert, 56–57
Military personnel, 8, 9, 26–29, 51–57
Milk contamination of, 8
  iodine-131 in, 77, 78
Mororoa, 49

Nagasaki, 20–21, 36, 97, 107
  atomic veterans at, 26–29
National Aeronautics and Space Administration, 86–87
National Association of Atomic Veterans (NAAV), 101, 102
National Association of Radiation Survivors (NARS), 100, 102
National Nuclear Ethics Law, 103

Nevada, 8, 20, 35–50
Nevada Proving Grounds, 36
Nevada Test Site (NTS), 36, 38, 42, 52, 93–97
New Zealand, 49–50, 107
North Korea, 34, 108
Nuclear arsenal, U. S., 36
Nuclear material, radiation in, 10
Nuclear Nonproliferation Treaty (NPT), 107
Nuclear power, radiation in, 10
Nuclear Regulatory Commission (NRC), 90
Nuclear testing, 7–11, 23–33, 34, 74–75
Nuclear waste, radiation in, 10
Nuclear workers, 20

Oak Ridge, TN, 25
O'Leary, Hazel, 86, 103, 104

Pacific, testing in, 48, 49
Parowan, UT, 71
Pauling, Linus, 72–73
Plutonium, 8, 9, 17, 48, 72, 83–87
Plutonium-239, 15
Polynesia, French, 107
Prenatal problems, as caused by radiation, 7
President's Advisory Committee on Human Radiation Experiments, report of, 86–87
Public Health Administration, experiments of, 86
Public Health Service, 76, 77, 78, 82

Rad, defined, 17
Radiation, 7, 10, 14–21, 27–29, 45–46, 47, 73–75, 93–97
Radiation-exposed Veterans Act of 1988, 100
Radiation Exposure Compensation Act, 100, 103

Radioactive particles, 7–8
Radionuclides, 16
Rainbow Warrior, 50
Rainbow Warrior II, 107
Rainier Mesa, 47
Rainout, 31
Rem, defined, 17
Roentgen, 17
Rongerik Island, 30

St. George, UT, 38, 39, 41, 44, 57, 58, 72, 95
Sheep, 62–70, 91–92
Sievert, defined, 17
South Pacific, 20, 60–61
Sovereign immunity, doctrine of, 88–89, 94, 98
Soviet Union, 9–10, 33, 46, 48, 49, 105, 106
Sternglass, Ernest, 45, 73
Strontium, 8
Strontium-90, 46, 76
Subcommittee on Oversight and Investigation, 90–91
Subcommittee on Public Health and the Environment, 90

Taylor, JoAnn, 39–40
Test ban, treaties toward, 105–9
Testing, 37–38, 46–47, 48–50, 51–52
  See also Atomic testing; Nuclear testing
Thyroid cancer, 45, 99, 100
  prevalence of, 81, 82
Trinity test, 23–25
Truman, Harry S., 23–24, 29, 33, 35, 36, 42
Truman, Jay, 71–72

U-235, 14, 73
  See also Uranium

U-238, 15
  See also Uranium
Udall, Stewart, 93, 97, 104
Underground testing, 46–48
  approval of, 105
United Kingdom, 46, 48–49, 105, 106, 107, 108
United Nations, 30, 50
U.S. Congress, investigations of, 9, 68
U.S. Court of Appeals, 92
U.S. Environmental Monitoring and Support Laboratory, 78
U.S. government
  admits guilt, 8
  duplicity of, 90
  failure of, to detect radiation, 27–29
  justification of, for nuclear testing, 34
  as nuclear power, 107
  nuclear tests of, 7–11, 23–33
  and plutonium experiments, 83, 84–85
  and test ban treaty, 106
  testings of, 46–47, 48, 49, 105, 108
Uranium, 8, 14–15, 17, 48
Utah, 8, 81–82

Veterans Administration, 54, 57, 80, 98–99
Veterans Administration Board of Appeals, 99

Warner Amendment, 99
Warren, Shields, 37, 53
Washington County, UT, 44, 71, 76, 81
Weiss, Edward, 76–77, 78

Yield, measurement of, 14